AF657544

THE SOCIAL STRUCTURE OF AN INDIAN VILLAGE

THE SOCIAL STRUCTURE OF AN INDIAN VILLAGE

N. K. SHUKLA
Reader & Head of the
Post Graduate Department of Sociology
Bhagalpur University

COSMO PUBLICATIONS
NEW DELHI ● INDIA
1976

First Published 1976
© N. K. SHUKLA, 1976

Published by
Rani Kapoor (Mrs.)
Cosmo Publications
24B, Ansari Road, Daryaganj
New Delhi-110002

Printed at
Rakesh Press
Naraina Industrial Area
New Delhi-110028

PREFACE

This book has grown out of my Doctoral Dissertation which was accepted by the Ranchi University in the year 1968. I thank my University for sanction of financial assistance and grant of study leave which increasingly enabled me to undertake the field work in Bharko and write the thesis at Bhagalpur.

It is indeed a matter of great pleasure for me to express my sincerest feelings of indebtedness and gratitude to Professor L.P. Vidyarthi, M.A. (Luck); Ph.D. (Chicago); F.A.A.A; Head of the Post-Graduate Department of Anthropology and President, The 10th International Congress of Anthropological and Ethnological Sciences, Ranchi University, whose scholarly guidance, constant supervision, valuable suggestions and affectionate encouragements helped me immensely in the completion of thesis. So kind and affectionate he is to me that he has further favoured me by writing a Foreword to this book for which I wish to thank him and express again my appreciation and obligations to him.

My thanks are also due to the officials of the Block, the village Panchayat and the village Karmachari who supplied me unhesitatingly necessary factual information, papers and documents. I am equally obliged to the people of Bharko for the honest and sincere co-operation which they extended to me on all occasions while I was staying in the village.

I shall be failing in my duty if I do not thank the Headmaster of the Village High School who not only made my stay safe and convenient in the village but also rendered unstinted help during the course of field work.

My junior colleague, Mr. R.R.P. Singh and five of my Post-Graduate students assisted me in the collection of data for which I thank them all. Mr. Gopal Prasad Ambastha, Senior Stenographer and my office assistant, Mr. B.P. Sinha, Bhagalpur University, deserve thanks for the patience and care with which they have prepared type-script for this book.

Like many other researchers, I too relied heavily on the works of a number of eminent authors and writers on village studies. Several British, American and Indian Social Anthropologists and Sociologists have done valuable researches in differrent parts of 'Village India'. Since it is not possible to mention them all, only those scholars who deserve my special praise and appreciation and whose reference I have cited on more than one occasion in my book are to be named. They are — Prof. Redfield, Bailey, Opler, Mayer, Lewis, Mandelbaum, Marriott, Beals, M.N. Srinivas, S.C. Dube, D.N. Majumdar, L.P. Vidyarthi, Madan, Mathur, Pradhan, Chauhan and a host of others.

To Mrs. Rani Kapoor, Proprietor, Cosmo Publications, New Delhi, I am extremely grateful for her personal interest, care and attention which this book has received during the course of its publication.

Finally, it is really a pleasure to note my indebtedness and obligations to my wife, Bijoy Laxmi Shukla, one time lecturer in my Department, for her valuable suggestions, inspiration, ungrudging help and active co-operation.

9th June, 1976 N.K. SHUKLA

Department of Sociology
Bhagalpur University
Bhagalpur — 7

CONTENTS

FOREWORD

The publication of Dr. N.K. Shukla's book on the Social Structure of an Indian Village is a very welcome addition to the little explored field of social Anthropology of Bihar. It is unfortunate that during the fifties and sixties when several villages were studied by the Sociologists and Social Anthropologists in the different parts of India, Bihar lagged behind. Credit goes to Dr. Shukla to fill in this gap by undertaking an intensive field research in a typical village of South Bihar (Bharko), analysing data in terms of the latest theoretical frame to produce a micro-level implications about rural India.

The volume presents not only an ethnographic account of the village in terms of its unity and extension but also brings out the latest transformations that the village has witnessed under the impact of modern forces of change, especially, through the Community Development Programme, educational centres, the Panchayati Raj and other democratic experiments. The change in the intercaste relationship as well as the structure of authority and power in the village has found an insightful, objective and interpretative analysis.

In the light of substantive data he has brought out the emergence of two powerful castes (The Brahmins and the Yadavas) which has affected the traditional structure of authority and power and generated intercaste conflicts and tension, and thus, led to social instability in the village social organisation. He further goes to establish the weekening of the traditional authority of caste panchayat and established village-leadership, as well as the emergence of the lower-caste group in the fields of politics and economic rivalry.

The book is a very valuable contribution to the Social

Anthropology of Bihar in general and village study of South Bihar in particular.

17.7.1976

(L.P. Vidyarthi)
President
The Tenth World Anthropological
& Ethnological Congress. Dept. of
Anthropology, Ranchi University,
Ranchi, Bihar, India.

CHAPTER I

A Brief Survey of Village Studies

The development of research into village communities studied by sociologists and anthropologists, within and without the country, covers a period of nearly thirty years. Reflections on various facets of peasant life and culture appear even earlier in several impressive accounts of litterateurs, visitors, administrators, economists etc; but they are of little significance before well-organized and scientifically sound studies of modern villages. Today, interest in the subject in countries like U.K. and U.S.A. has gone very far with the accumulation of a good deal of facts and materials. Perhaps this poses a problem for a researcher interested in surveying the course of development of community studies conducted so far in many parts of the world and in different periods of history. Professor Vidyarthi (1966 : 8) in his brilliant paper on Social Anthropolitcal Researches in India presented to the VIIth International Congress for Anthropological and Ethnological Sciences held at Moscow studied for himself the development of anthropological researches in the country in three periods, namely, Formulatory period (1774-1919), Constructive period (1920-1950) and Analytical period (1950-)[1]. It is not my intention to outline the reasons for the seriousness of the problem. Here, I simply propose to give a brief and passing reference to some significant village studies with particular stress on those dealing with the Indian peasantry appearing in the period between 1936-1966.

The beginning of village studies is marked by the appearance of two outstanding works, namely—"Village Communities in the East and West" and "Village Communities in India" written by Sir Henry Maine and Badden-Powell respectively. These works, appearing toward the middle of the 19th century, have led much more to the close understanding of peasant society in its many-fold aspects — evolutionary, historical, political, economic and theoretical. The period is equally marked by observations on economic aspects of the community-land-tenure, settlement pattern and revenue system for the simple reason that economic organization and social structure of a village are interlinked. Village studies have hitherto remained the main concern of the economists and it is quite lately that anthropologists and sociologists, due to the developing nature of their subjects, have paid attention to the field.

The period between 1920-1936 or even beyond serves as a landmark in the annals of community studies as several outstanding thinkers and scholars, majority of them are from the United States and Great Britain, have made a number of valuable contributions to the close understanding of village communities. Notable among these thinkers and scholars are the following — Whitehead, George Briggs, Slater, Brayne, Wiser, William Henricks, Emerson, Young, M.L. Darling, Robert Redfield and others. The period witnesses a stream of publications on many aspects of community life of which the following deserve to be mentioned — Polish Peasant in Europe and America, Behind Mudwalls in India, Voiceless India, Middletown, Tepoztlan : A Mexican Village, Chankom : A Maya Village, Culture and civilization in a Guatemala Society.

Much more significant from theoretical and methodological standpoints are some more works appearing during the period ranging from 1940-1956. With their publication sufficient literature on the subject gets ready for availability to teachers and research-students, and the hope of exploring all aspects of community life materialises. A few revealing works include—Peasant Life in China, A Chinese Village, A Japanese Village,

A Sierra Tarascan Village, Transformation Scene, Quiroga : A Mexican Village. These fifteen years really constitute a wonderful period of development and progress and are singularly helpful in visualising the emergence of community studies as a special branch of study in social anthropology and rural sociology in India and elsewhere too. Social scientists, research workers, research organizations, educational institutions, Governmental machineries, plans and projects, journals, periodicals, all have gone to play their important roles during the period in exploring the hitherto neglected peasantry which "still constitutes almost threefourths of the world's peoples and make up the bulk of the population in the under-developed countries."[2] Oscar Lewis (1958 : VII).

The period from 1950 onward is especially significant in view of the huge mass of studies and researches both by American and Indian anthropologists and sociologists in the field. Among the foreigners who have done valuable researches on various aspects of Indian villages are the following :—

> Mandelbaum, W.M. Smith, F.G. Bailey, A.R. Beals, Morris Opler, Oscar Lewis, Mackim Marriott, Andrin Mayer, W.H. Newell, G.M. Carstairs, Eric Miller, Kathleen Gough, B.S. Cohn, G.P. Steed and others. Outstanding amomg Indian thinkers and scholars are M.N. Srinivas, S.C. Dube, D.N. Majumdar, R.K. Mookherjee, J. Sharma, I. Karve, R.N. Saxena, A.R. Desai, N.S. Reddy, Sridhar Mishra, Enayet Ahmed, Pradhan, K. Ishwaran, K.S. Mathur, T.N. Madan, Brij Raj Chauhan, L. P. Vidyarthi and others.

A list of important villages so far surveyed with names of States in the country is presented below :—

Sl. No.	*Name of States*	*Names of Villages*
1.	Delhi	Ranikhera, Rampur.
2.	Kashmir	Utrassa-Umanagri.
3.	Uttar Pradesh	Senapur,Kishangarhi,Madhopur.
4.	Rajasthan	Fatehpur, Dilwara, Ranawaton Ki — Sadri.
5.	Madhya Pradesh	Malwa.

6.	Gujarat	Kasandra.
7.	Bombay	Dharavi.
8.	Mysore.	Rampura, Namhalli, Hittalahalli, Shivapur.
9.	Kerala	Villages in Travancore-Cochin.
10.	Madras	Kumbapettai, TM.
11.	Andhra Pradesh	Shamirpet.
12.	Orissa	Bisipara and Mohanpur
13.	Bengal	A village in Hooghly.
14.	Bihar	Ghaghra.

In addition to the above, a survey of fourteen villages in the districts of Meerut and Bulandshahar in the State of Uttar Pradesh and in Hissar and Rohtak districts in the State of Haryana has been completed by Mukherjee and Gupta. A few villages in the States of Himachal Pradesh and Assam have also been studied. From these it can safely be established that village studies have now become an integral part of modern anthropological and sociological researches. In India, they have gained much importance particularly in the post-independence period. Also the Government is bound solemnly, morally, constitutionally and politically to improve the socio-economic condition of the rural people who still constitute nearly 70% to 80% of the country's total population. Perhaps all aspects of village communities, from stability to change have been covered; still some more discoveries are yet to be made in different geographical and cultural regions of the country.

A few edited books on Indian villages appear in the year 1955. These include, India's Villages by M.N Srinivas, Village India by Marriott and Rural Profiles by D.N. Majumdar. Articles contained in these books have originally been published in Economic weekly, American Anthropologist, American Sociological Review and in several other research journals. Dube's "Indian Village" published in the same year is indeed a valuable piece of research work, devoted to the study of social and cultural aspects of the people of Shamirpet. Oriented towards the study of social change is his another work "India's Changing Villages". Srinivas's "Religion and Society Among the Coorgs of South India" (1952) is a masterpiece of analysis and description. Besides, "Social Change In Modern India" (1966), "Caste in Modern India & other Essays" (1962) etc. are his other works valuable for their presentation of a number of concepts. Some more recent books on the life and culture of Indian rural communities include — Politics and Social Change : Orissa in 1959 by F.G Bailey (1963), Village Life In Northern India (1958) by Oscar Lewis, Caste and Communication in an Indian Village (1958) by D.N. Majumdar, Caste and Ritual in a Malwa Village (1964) by K.S. Mathur, Dusk and Dawn in Village India (1965) by Zahir Ahmed, Family And Kinship (1965) by T.N. Madan, Tradition and Economy In Village India (1966) by K. Iswaran, A Rajasthan Village (1967) by Brij Raj Chauhan, Ghaghra (1961) by L.P. Vidyarthi, Social Economy of a Polyandrous People (1962) by R.N. Saxena and many others.

Quite a part from these, a number of research journals continue to maintain progress in this direction. Research articles are often published in Eastern Anthropologist, Indian Journal of Agricultural Economics, Kurukshetra, Man in India, Rural India, Rural Sociology, Social Forces and Sociological Bulletin. Among the agencies championing the cause of village studies in under-developed countries by way of lending financial support are — UNESCO, Ford Foundation, Social Science Research Council, Planning Commission, besides Universities providing scholarships and fellowships.

A number of research projects are in action under the supervision of well experienced professors and scholars in Universities and research institutes within and without the country. The Cornell group headed by Prof. Opler and another team led by Prof. Lewis, in response to a request from the Programme Evaluation Organization, have done appreciable work on peasant life in the country and created an indelible interest and urge in the minds of Indian scholars, administrators, planners and policy makers to do their utmost in the assessment of the problems of village communities. On the basis of these achievements we may now hope to offer scientific solutions to multifarious problems ranging from gnawing poverty to appalling indebtedness of the villagers, with a view to ensuring them a better future in the years to come.

Social Structure Defined

The concept to social structure has occupied an important place almost from the very beginning. The term has been largely used in the writings of Herbert Spencer, Durkheim, Mannheim and invariably in modern literature. Notwithstanding well developed meanings, it is still frequently used in its wider connotation, referring to any or all features contributing to the make-up of societies. It thus becomes a synonym for system, organization, pattern, type and indeed does not fall very short of society as a whole.[3] S.F. Nadel (1957 : 2). Morris Ginsberg (1947 : 8) observes, "Social structure is concerned with the principal form of social organization, i.e., types of groups, associations and institutions and the complex of these which constitute societies."[4] According to MacIver and Page (1962 : 209) "Group structures represent the kind of reality into which we are born and within which we find work and recreation, rewards and penalties, struggle and mutual aid".[5] But Kaplan (1957 : 88) on personality and social structure uses the term social structure to indicate the over-all organization of social institutions and other components of the social system.[6]

Now let us know the views of some more thinkers on social structure. Bottomore (1962 : 111) endorses the contention of Ginsberg and regards social structure as a complex of the major institutions and groups in society. He outlines five minimum requirements of a social system :

(1) a sytem of communication ;

(2) an economic system ;

(3) arrangements (including the family and education) for the socialization of new generations ;

(4) a sytem of authority and of distribution of power; and

(5) a system of ritual.[7]

According to Johnson, structure of a social system includes :

(1) subgroups of various types, interconnected by relational norms ;

(2) roles of various types ;

(3) regulative norms governing subgroups and roles ; and

(4) cultural values.

Anderson and Parker maintain that "all men live with other men in societies and that these societies are entities composed of human relationship structures. This is to say that each society has a pattern of organization composed of the structures resulting from the association of men with each other".[8] Anderson & Parker (1964 : 89)

There are still some more thinkers and scholars who have given their own interpretation of the concept. For instance, Talcott Parsons, while making a classification of possible types of social structure and complementary role definitions says "the structure of a social system is essentially the structure relations between actors in interaction", whereas, for Merton, social structure comprises the patterned arrangements of role-sets, status-sets and status-sequences.

In the field of anthropology, the concept has been used specifically in its developed and redefined meanings. Radcliffe-Brown (1964 : 191) explains that the components of social structure are human beings; the structure itself being an arrangement of person in relationship institutionally defined and regulated. In the study of social structure the concrete reality with which we are concerned is the set of actually existing relations, at a given moment of time, which link together certain human beings.[9]

Eggan finds the components or units of social structure in the inter-personal relations, whereas Evans Pritchard restricts the use of the concept to inter-relations of groups. For Raymond Firth, social structure is social alignment or the ordering of the personnel component of the community.

From the aforesaid observations it follows that the concept of social structure entails polemic discussions and any attempt to discover uniformity would prove to be futile. It is better to endorse the views of Robert Redfield whose observation is, "Social structure is the holistic concept: the central organizing idea in terms of which everything else in the life of a community so far as proves possible is seen."[10] Redfield (1955 : 49). The concept has been used throughout in this thesis in a broad sense combining elements like family and kinship, groups and institutions, authority and power, religion and caste, education and economy.

SOCIAL STRUCTURE OF A VILLAGE

Many a British and American anthropologist has described village communities in terms of social structure, and thus, the use of the concept for the whole of a community is well-known to everyone. In the treatment of social structure one has to focus one's attention on the relationship man or put particular stress on the Corporate groups of the community. Similarly, for understanding the Social Structure of an Indian village, apart from the study of its relationships and group structure, we have to view it as a community within communities, though in the pattern of inter-group adjustment this may be that the village retains slightly its individual character.

Against this background let us analyse the stable elements in the social structure of a village. The village exhibits a number of salient features as parts of its social structure. The first and the most important is the family nuclear or compound or joint which is the basic society of the community. Everyone belongs to a family and is known to the co-villagers due to kinship and lineage relationships. Individual members of the family perform certain functions and fulfil obligations towards one another. These actions of the members interlock them into different relationships, which constitute an important element in the social structure of the viilage.

Another important part of the community's social structure is the caste system. Caste exists as a rigid and ossified social institution determining and regulating the behaviour of members in myriad ways. Caste is hereditary and fixes one's position and status in the community. It serves as an agency of transmitting culture and skills peculiar to each of its groups to which are also tied separate occupations. It does not only reflect the horizontal strata but also determines the area of of marriage along with certaian taboos and religious duties for each of the members.

The village panchayat which is now the custodian of authority and power is equally an important element into which social structure of the community is organized. Its usefulness in the organization of inter-personal and intercaste relations as well as the solutions of quarrels and disputes arising in the village is very great. The traditional panchayat is no longer in operation; instead, new elected panchayat working on democratic tradition and decentralization of power has come into being.

Again, rituals and ceremonies are the other traits which the village manifests as part of its social structure. It has been observed by Sir Harcourt Butler quoted by Lewis that "The Indians are essentially religious as the Europeans are essentially secular. Religion is still the alpha and omega of Indian life."[11] Oscar Lewis (1958 : 249). The village is still under the stronghold of religion and rituals which shape and colour the life and destinies of its people in many ways. In the villages they still exercise their powerful influence in controlling and regulating the behaviour of its members. Rituals and ceremonies are essentially held as promoting co-operation, harmony and integration in the rural areas. The village is distinctly characterised by the 'great' and 'little' traditions of Hinduism.

Though the study of economic institutions is the principal concern of the economists, the village economy, as part of its social system, ought to be analysed by an anthropologist or a sociologist in order to review the relationship between the system of economic distribution of goods and services and the social organization of the village. A survey of the type of agriculture, livestock, the economic functions of caste, economic classes etc; will focus light on the social structure of the village. Innovations and several other changes have utterly broken the self-sufficiency of the village economy and given it a place in the national economy. The village, therefore, does not simply function as a unit of production and consumption but as a unit of distribution and exchange too.

Lastly, norms and values, education and affiliation of the village to external influences are the additional features which ought to be analysed in the context of social structure. Likewise, the influence of leadership on the internal administration and organization of the village serves as an important link in the study of the social structure of the village community. From the description of social structure, the study of certain new alterations and modifications, whether gradual or sudden, major or minor, in the structure and organization of the village, is the main highlight of the present research.

Village Communities : A Historical Review

Although, in the past, village communities in India adopted diverse and hetrogeneous patterns of existence and development, yet some kind of basic similarity was discernible among them throughout the Sothern and Northern regions of the country. This very fundamental truth about India's physical and cultural unity has been discovered by Dr. R. K. Mookherjee (1950 : 61) —"This distinctive Indian culture in course of time so far unified the country that the country and the culture came to be identified and became synonymous terms. The country was the culture and the culture the country, the kingdom of spirit, transcending to territorial limits".[12] In this section, it is proposed to present, quite in a nutshell, a historical account of the development of village communities in India.

Vedic Period—(2000 B.C.—1000 B.C.)

Sir Charles Metcalfe (1832 : 331) expressed his views about village communities in India in this manner : "The village communities are little republics, having nearly everything they want within themselves and almost independent of any foreign relations. They seem to last where nothing else lasts. Dynasty after dynasty tumble down. Revolution succeeds revolution but the village community remains the same. This union of village communities, each one forming a separate little state in itself, has contributed more than any other cause to the preservation of the people of India".[13] The views of Metcalfe, in the eyes of a few eminent historians including Dr. A. S. Altekar, were found valid alone for the Vedic period but not for the subsequent periods.

The Vedas, particularly the Rig-Veda, described clearly as to how the village, as a basic and fundamental unit, shared much of the responsibilities in the organization of Indian social polity. Villages enjoyed the status of small independent republics, and the Samiti, that of a common assembly of the entire people, fostering in them the feelings of liberty, equality and fraternity. Gramini or Chief of the Village and Gram Sabha or village council were the most important units of the administrative machinery. The society as a whole was adequately developed and well-settled, characterised by differentiation of functions and combination of bodies, namely, Kula, Jana, Jati, Puga, Vrata, Sreni, Sangha, Samudaya, Samuha, Sambhuyar-Samutthana, Parishad, Charana etc. The Mahabharat made prominent mention of village system and inter-village organization. The epic distinguished two types of villages on the basis of size, namely, (i) the Ghosh and (ii) the Grama. The former was smaller than the latter generally situated near the forestland. Besides the Gramini, who was an overall incharge of the village administration, there were other officials next to him, for example, (1) Das-Gramini—over 10 villages; (2)Vim-Satipa—over 20 villages; (3) Satgramini or Gram-Satadhyaksha — over 100 villages; and (5) Adhipati — over 1000 villages. Sri H. D. Malaviya (1956: 45: 46) gave a vivid description of the village in ancient India and its officials. The Ramayan also classified the village into Ghosh and Gram whose officials were the Ghosh-Mahattar and Gram-Mahattar. Manu, the erudite scholar of Hindu law, described the village official as Gramik whose responsibilities were : (a) the administration of the village; (b) collection of state dues; (c) village defence; (d) maintenance of records. In addition to Gramik, the other senior officials included: (1) Dasi—over 10 villages; (2) Vishanti—over 20 villages: (3) Shati or Sat-Gramadhipati—over 100 villages; and (4) Shasta-Gramadhi-Pati — over 1000 villages[14].

Buddhist Period (500 *B. C.—200 B. C.*)

Throughout the Buddhist and Jain periods one would find several references to various types of human settlements. The Buddhist literature elaborately referred to the arrangement of villages, towns and forts. According to Dr. R. K. Mookherjee (1950 : 299 : 301) the Buddhist texts made possible divisions of human habitation into grama, nigama, kula and nagarka whereas the Jain tests recognized grama, ghosha, kheta, karvata, palli, pattana, samvaha, matamba etc. as the important types of human settlements.[15] Other aspects of the village like dwellings, land area, land holding, village common and boundary were also included in the description.

Maurya Period

Kautilya in his famous Artha Shastra gave some-what similar descriptions of sites, boundary and organization of villages in the period. The striking feature was the intervillage organization into units or unions. A union of 100 villages was known as Samgrahana; of 200 villages as Karvati; 500 villages as Dronamukha and of 800 villages as Mahagrama or administratively as Sthatnuja, i.e., the modern Thana or Police station.

According to Sri K. D. Malaviya, villages during the time of Chandra Gupta Maurya were divided into three types. viz, Jyestha or the biggest, Madhyama or the middling and Kanishtha or the smallest. These were further classified into — (1) Gramagras or simple villages paying usual revenues; (2) Pariharak or revenue-free villages, generally given to the priest for the spread of education and Dharma among the people; (3) Ayudhuja or revenue-free village for supply of men when needed for recruitment as soldiers, and, lastly, villages which paid revenue in the shape of agricultural produce.[16] H. D. Malaviya (1956 : 72 : 73 :)

Muslim Period

Village communities began to witness, slowly but steadily, a tremendous change in the period due to what Dr. Altekar observed as 'internal and external forces'. The Vedic Sabha did not cxist in the Brahmanical age, and the Village Council, Council of Elders and the Village Panchayat which excited people's administration, had their powers immensely curtailed in the Muslim period. If somehow or other, they managed to exist, they continued to function as obsolete bodies. The institution of village headman grew fully. Of course, the headman acted as a man of the people rather than as an agency of the state.[17] G. R. Madan (1959:6)

British Period

The period witnessed the introduction of new policies and systems of administration which caused the village communities a great setback and village institutions' complete disappearance. Dr. Altekar describes the scene of transformation "The British influence, dominant and all-sided, has all but killed most of the village institutions. The headman has lost his importance; the lekhakar or accountant has ceased to be hereditary; the village council no longer exists; the Panchayat is never heard of; the village fund had also vanished. The theory therefore that the Indian village communities do not change is completely disapproved by the teachings of history."[18]

Even a cursory glance at the past — beginning from the Vedic period down to the British, would reveal the fact about immense changes occurring inwardly among Indian village communities. The Indian village, in the context of a larger society, continued to exist as a basic social structure of the rural aggregates and would remain so in the future except with its shape and form tremendously changed. Isolation and stagnation were the past characteristics of the village but these no longer persist. It is instability and internal influence than anything else which, for the most part, characterise the village in contemporary India

Village Communities : A Modern Review

What does the village signify in contemporary India ? Into what possible types can villages be classified ? Are they static or in the process of vast transformations the country has ushered in ? What structural and organizational similarity or dissimilarity can be discovered among them ? And, to what extent do they portray the changing patterns of Indian culture and society ? These are important issues which deserve consideration in the scientific and systematic study of 'Indian Village'. An effort will be made to provide answers to these questions.

Harold J.E. Peake describes "The village community consists of group of related or unrelated persons larger than a Single family, occupying a large house or a number of dwellings placed close together, sometimes irregularly, sometimes in a street, and cultivating, originally in common, a number of arable fields, dividing the available meadowland between them and pasturing their cattle upon the surrounding waste land, over which the community claims rights as for as boundaries of adjacent communities."[19] Robert Refield (1958:4) outlines the meanings of a little community as distinctiveness, homogeneity smallness and all-providing self-sufficiency and, above all, "a cradle-to-the-grave arrangement."[20] Much of the ingredients contained in the definition are obtainable in the existing state of affairs but they may not in all respects be applicable to nearly more than half a million villages in India. Besides the statistical definition emphasizing the number of inhabitants and the use of the concept interchangeably for a tiny collection of huts or a larger hamlet or a big village, the village at the present moment means a collection of huts and houses, most of them are either mudbuilt or thatched or roofed wtih locally made tiles with fields lying all around. Narrow streets or otherwise used for passage and mutual relationship, self-sufficiency, unity and solidarity in internal affairs are some of its other features.

Villages differ from each other in several respects. Besides social and cultural variations, regional and local differences, are also conspicuously found among them. For instance, the social system of Dr. Cohn's Madhopur differs markedly from that of Kathleen Gough's Kumbapettai or villages described by Dr. Srinivas and Dr. Dube are quite diffierent from those studied by Dr, Opler and Dr. Lewis. Obviously villages in North Bihar will be quite different in certain respects from those in South Bihar. Similarly the village under study fails to indentify itself in many respects with those studied by Bailey or in other parts of the country. Thus there are countless cases in which they are found to have differed from each other. The degree of differences prevailing among them can be known if certain criteria like size, caste, landholding, degree of external influence, authority, power etc. are carefully employed and examined. Just as nucleated or compact villages differ from dispersed villages or joint villages from severalty villages or centrally situated villages from round villages and street villages from entirely shapeless villages, similarly, in respect of each of the aforesaid criteria, villages would exhibit striking differences.

It is a simple truth that villages whose population is in terms of hundred would be smaller in size than those whose population is in terms of thousand. Similarly a village, which represents several castes including the Muslims, will be considered as complex in respect of its structure and organization than that which has a minimum number of castes. Again, a village, which has the dominance of one or more castes as in the case of Bharko—the village under study—will be different from that which has no such dominance. The economic and social value of land gives it a unique position in the life of thé community. If land is concentrated in one to two families or one to two castes in a particular village, the organization of this village will surely be different from that where the same is widely distributed. Likewise the village, which is in close proximity to the influence of industrial urbanism or the city or having easy communication, will present a different scene than that which is interior and isolated. Bailey describes : "In more technical terms, Mohanpur is more closely integrates with the larger society, whereas Bisipara has a high degree of internal integration and externally is isolated."[21]

Today, villages have ceased to be independent, self-sufficient and autonomous in the wider sense of the term. However, in certain domestic and internal affairs or arrangements they maintain the independent and autonomous character. As the locus of power helps in understanding the ways of the operation of village-organization, it should be known whether the same is concentrated in a few big land-holders (as zamindars do not exist after the abolition of the system in this State and elsewhere too) or the village Panchayat or the dominant caste. Each caste has its own cultural heritage and, in that sense, acts independently of other castes. While caste prescriptions find expression in the behaviour of the members, conformity to prevailing usages, norms and values in a large measure accounts for the differences among villages. Owing to some regional and local variations in culture, certain contrasting and disassociative processes are ostensible among the villages such as co-operation, conflict, notoriety, meanness, peacefulness and these cause differences in their structural and organizational framework.

To-day villages are in the process of change and transformation. The introduction of mordern forces has greatly contributed to accelerate this process and to bring about immense changes in several important aspects of the village. Change is discernible in the joint family system which has headed towards its disintegration and its gradual replacement by elementary family, consisting of husband, wife and the unmarried children. Similarly, except the hereditary and endogamous character of caste which the village still retains, its other aspects, for which it existed in the past, are undergoing gradual changes. The introduction of newly elected panchayats in most of the States avowed with legal and constructive functions is the modern outcome of the democratic tradition and decentralization of power. The process in the the accomplishment of the 'great' and 'little' traditions of Hinduism and its collusion with the so-called modernity results in the emergence of readjustment of patterns in the religious life of the villagers. Innovations and new changes have threatened the economic self-sufficiency of the village and determined its place in the national economy. Outside contact with towns and cities have widened the cultural outlook of the people in the rural areas. Villages are gradually taking to urban character.

Field Work :

Bharko, the village under study, is situated at a distance of 22 miles to the south-west of Bhagalpur in the State of Bihar. It so happened that I heard of the village from two of my post-graduate students who, in fact, hailed from the place. For the first time in the year 1964 I had the opportunity of going over there in connection with the supervision of research project of my Department. A few days of my stay in the village were enough to develop curiosity and interest in village studies. The present research is partly an outcome of my pre-developed motivation.

The actual field work for the thesis started from March to July and again from September to December in 1966 i.e. for a total period of nine months. One of my colleagues and five students assisted me in the data collection work but I myself did the major part of it. Field work in the rural area is really a stupendous task especially for the outsiders who are often received with an attitude of indifference and non-co-operation. It is needless to emphasize the difficulties, which I encountered in the field work, which were not solved by the mere establishment of so-called rapport or the use of various techniques and skills but chiefly by having a long enduring patience. The hardship was so great that the work had to be suspended on two occasions. Illiteracy and cultural backwardness continued to obstruct the work till its completion.

According to the census of India, 1951, there are altogether 71,378 villages in the State of Bihar and out of this number, 17,389 villages come under the South Bihar.[22] Therefore, it is difficult to comprehend how a single village can represent the total range of diversity found in the whole of the State. Bharko. was selected as a sample village representing sufficient number of castes, occupations and population. The work started with the gathering of population statistics on the basis of family register followed by a door-to-door survey.

The Panchayat records available with the Gram Sewak and the Karmachari records were carefully studied for demographic, economic and certain social statistics. Out of a total of 433 families in the village, a sample of 300 families was selected for an exclusive study of family,caste, religion, ritual, income and expenditure. The most commonly used methods of schedule and questionnaire along with the techniques of interview and participant observer were employed for the purpose. Attitude and opinion regarding caste factions, group leaders, intercaste and inter-personal relations, rules of exogamy and endogamy, panchayat, rituals and ceremonies were carefully studied and analysed. Many more helpful information were gathered from case study of 50 families in addition to those secured from life history of 20 persons. All possible efforts have been made to present an uncluttered account of the social structure and, as far as possible, facts and figures used in the thesis have been carefully verified with the available records. It is a pity that there is no uniformity in the statistics provided by the Karamchari, Gram Sewak and the V. L. W. As far as practicable, I relied mostly on my personal investigation; however, my dependence on the Panchayat records was reasonably unavoidable.

Application of Concepts

There was long-drawn controversy over the question of the use of methods for studying village communities. The issue ultimately led to the emergence of two schools of thought—one was represented by a group of British, including a few American anthropologists and the other wholly by a group of American anthropologists. The former viewed village communities as isolated wholes within themselves, whereas the latter maintained that they were parts of a larger whole. Both the approaches appeared quite convincing in their proportionate degrees of abstraction and they influenced a number of thinkers and scholars in several parts of the world. However, as for myself, I would subscribe to the views of the second school.

Today, the concept of an isolated whole for an Indin rural community has been found to be inadequate and inappropriate. It may hold good to a tribal community which lies in the remotest part, unaffected by and cut off from the rest of the world. But there also it has its limited application. Redfield and Singer have questioned the description of village communities as isolated wholes whose life is constantly modified by other communities and into which institutions and offices are imported. "What forms of thought are available to us for conceiving and describing a whole that is both enclosed within other wholes and is also in some part permeated by them ?" — is the pertinent question which Redfield puts to us.

The first-hand impression, which a casual observer develops about the structure of a village, is that it is a distinct whole; but the truth comes out only after an analysis of each of the component elements or the sub-systems. Not to speak of little communities of the Western countries as isolated wholes which are closely imbedded in urban civilization, even the Indian villages are the part and parcel of the great Hindu tradition which exists outside them. If villages are imagined as isolated wholes and inclosed within themselves, what arguments do we have for policies like landtenure, collection of revenue, land mortgage, court cases etc. which used to be imported into them from time to time. This may be held valid except for South Indian villages, as some thinkers have conceived, where caste, kinship, and marital relations are localized. Even the present village fails to give any proof of its being conceived as an isolated whole for it maintains contact with other regions outside it through kinship, marriage, caste, economy, religion and party affiliation.

The question of whole and part relationship has further been analysed in terms of a few well-developed concepts. These are :—

(a) Evans-Pritchard's — structural distance
(b) Starr's – levels of communal relations
(c) Hanseen's Activity field
(d) Steward's levels of socio-cultural integration
(e) Marriott's — Universalization and Parochialization; and
(f) certain concepts of Redfield and Singer.

The concept of structural distance enables me to discover types of concentric groups differing in various degrees found within and outside the village. Three such types of communities are distinguishable in the village. They are :—

(1) a hamlet over which Bharko exercises political and cultural supremacy;

(2) Three neighbouring villages, somewhat independent and equal in status as well as in importance which lie outside Bharko and with which the people of Bharko are interlocked with the ties of caste, kinship and marriage; and

(3) a group of villages falling under the region having linguistic and cultural similarity with the village.

The concept of communal relations helps me to view Bharko as related not only to its people but equally to other 'levels' existing outside the village. These levels are neighbouring villages joined by inter-village organization, town, region, state etc. with successive degrees of relationships at different stages. The concept also helps to understand that social relations become more impersonal and subjected to the principle of subordination and super-ordination as one moves towards other levels. The smaller groups with which Bharko maintains direct and personal contact are subordinated to it in certain respects where as Bhorko itself is subjected to the super-ordination of its larger groups like towns and cities with which it is indirectly and formally linked.

The concept of activity field not only makes me realise Bharko's ties with the world outside but at the same time makes it understandable that a similarity exists between the activity field and structural distance. Also it helps me to visualise a few economically and socially distinct groups as are obtainable in towns and cities functioning smoothly in the village under study. As for example, the activities and relationships of a land-owning class differ from those of a landless class. It is difficult to discover the influence of specific activities and relationships or towns and cities operating in the village except that the same can be explained in terms of rural urban continuum of a general import. In its sphere of trade and business the village is influenced by towns and cities although the urbanites hardly trade in the village inspite of its famous weekly market in which grain, cattle, vegetables, clothes and other commodities of daily use are sold and purchased. Of course, only people from neighbouring villages and a few distant villages, but not from towns and cities, come to the weekly market.

Today, Indian villages are linked directly or indirectly, for various political and administrative purposes, with the State and Central Governments. Policies and laws of the Government bind the villagers more today than in the past as is evident from the abolition of zamindari system, survey settlement, collection of revenue and levy, irrigation and power, village panchayat, development block etc.

The concept of socio-cultural integration provides ways for dividing horizontal segments or levels in the village. The concept of primary civilization as distinct from secondary civilization is a continuous process going out of the folk culture with which the village is closely linked. Primary civilization leads to the development of great tradition which enriches itself with the cultural norms and values already contained in its local traditions. There is a constant communication between great and little traditions through sacred literature, geography, rituals and ceremonies. Viewed from the concept of great tradition of the primary civilization, Bharko seems to possess constant touch with the sacred literature, rituals and ceremonies of Hinduism and, in this respect, the village is enclosed within a larger whole.

Dominant Caste

The concept of dominant caste propounded by M.N. Srinivas has been aptly utilized in the thesis. Factors or elements responsible for the preponderance of a caste or castes which he has analysed in his study of Rampura are increasingly applicable to Bharko. Not only in the village but also in the neighbouring areas consisting of five to seven villages, the Yadavas are strongest and preponderate. Of course, the Brahmins have recently emerged as the second dominant caste in Bharko but compared to the Yadavas their position is much more inferior.

Professor Srinivas illustrates the concept "A caste is dominant when it is numerically and politically the strongest in the village or local area, and economically and politically exercises a preponderating influence. It need not be the highest caste in terms of traditional and conventional ranking of castes. The situation described by Dr. Gough for Kumbapettai is no longer typical. Any caste may be the dominant caste in an area though I have not come across the Untouchables being dominant anywhere... The point that is important here is that the dominant caste supports and maintains the total system. The dominant caste respects the code of every caste even when some features of it are different from the code of the dominant caste. Disputes occurring among the non-dominant castes are occasionally taken to the elders of the dominant caste".[23]

The concept has elaborately and adequately been developed except that it lacks in consistency and clarity.

Dr. D. N. Majumdar and others have also analysed and tested the concept in their study of Gohanakallan and Mohana villages.[24] Systematically the fatcors and elements which help a particular caste in its dominance are the following :—

(a) Numerical strength of the Caste

(b) Economic and political dominance

(c) Traditional superior status of a caste, and

(d) Administration of justice, unity and welfare of the Community as a whole.

Further, the social structure of a village dominated by a backward or untouchable caste does not make much headway economically, socially and culturally. In such situations social relations become embittered as the upper caste of village always endeavours and struggles to gain economic and political strength. Caste tensions are the product of urban political influence but that which works in the village emanates from the conventional terrestial divisions of caste.

As stated earlier, the Yadavas (who belong to the backward fold of the Hindu Caste) are numerically, economically, socially and politically the strongest in Bharko.

REFERENCES

CHAPTER I

1. Vidyarthi, L. P., 1966, *Social Anthropological Researches in India*—Journal of Social Research, Vol. IX—No. 1, March, (Council of Social and Cultural Research, Bihar and Department of Anthropology Ranchi University, Ranchi).

2. Lewis Oscar, 1958, *Village Life in Northern India*, (University of Illinois Press, Urbana).

3. Nadel, S.F., 1957, *The Theory of Social Structure*, (Cohen & West Ltd; Broadway House, 68-74 Carter Lane, London, E.C. 4).

4. Ginsberg, M., 1947, *Reason And Unreason in Society*, (William Heinemenn Ltd; London).

5. Maclver, R.M. & Page, C.H., 1962, Society : *An Introductory Analysis*, Macmillan & Co. Ltd; London).

6. Kaplan, B., 1957, "*Personality and Social Structure*"—Review of Sociology, Ed. by J.B. Gittler, (John Wiley & Sons, INC, New York.)

7. Bottomore, T.B., 1962, *Sociology—A Guide to Problems & Literature*, (George Allen & Unwin, Ltd; Ruskin House, London).

8. Anderson, W.A. & Parker, F.B., 1964, *Social Organization*, (D. Van Nostrand Company, INC, New York).

9. Redcliff-Brown, 1964, *Structure And Function in Primitive Society*, (The English Language Book Society & Cohen & West Ltd; London).

10. Redfield, Robert, 1955, *The Little Community*, (The University of Chicago Press, Chicago).

11. *Ibid*

12. Mookerji, R. K., 1950, *Hindu Civilization*, (Bhartiya Vidya Bhawan, Bombay).

13. Metcalfe, Sir Charless, 1832, *Report of the Select Committee of the House of Commons*, Vol. III, Appendix 84, Quoted by M.N. Srinivas in '*India's Villages*', Development, (Department, Government of West Bengal,) 1955. P. 21.

14. Malavia, H.D., 1956, *Village Panchayats in India*, (Economic & Political Dept., All India Congress Committee, New Delhi).

15. Malaviya, H.D., 1956, *Village Panchayats in India*, (Economic & Political Department, All India Congress Committee, New Delhi).

16. *Ibid.*

17. Madan, G.R., 1959, *Changing Pattern of Indian Villages*, (S. Chand & Co; Delhi).

18. Altekar, A.S., *Village Communities in Western India*, Quoted by A.R. Desai in Rural Sociology in India, (Vora & Co. Publishers (Private) Ltd; Bombay,) 1959, P. 196, P. 162,

19. Peake, H.J.E., 1935, *Encyclopaedia of the Social Sciences*, Vol. XV, 1935 P. 253.

20. Peake, H.J.E., 1935, *Encyclopaedia of the Social Sciences Vol.* XV, 1935, P. 253.

21. Bailey, F.G., 1963, *Politics and Social Change in Orissa in* 1959, (University of California Press).

22. Gopalaswami, R.A., 1951, *Census of India, Vol. I, Part—II A*, 1955, P. 6, (Manager of Publications, Delhi).

23. *Ibid.*

24. Srinivas, M.N., 1955, *India's Villages Development Department*, Government of West Bengal, Page 7.

25. 1955, Srinivas, M.N., *The Social System of a Mysore Village*, Village India, ed. by Mckim Marriott, (University of Chicago), P. 17-19.

26. Srinivas, M.N., 1959, *Social Change in India.*

27. Srinivas, M.N. 1959, *The Dominant Caste in Rampur*—American Anthropologist, Vol. 61, No. 1, Feb. 1959, Reprint P 1-10.

28. Majumdar, D.N., 1955, *Rural Profiler, The Ethnographic And Folk Culture Society*, Lucknow University, Lucknow, U.P. India, Page VIII.

CHAPTER II

Historical Perspective

The Setting

Bharko is situated at a distance of 22 miles to the South-West of Bhagalpur. Administratively, Bhagalpur forms the head-quarter of the Commissioner of the Division and is situated at the bank of the sacred Ganges.[1] O'Mallay (1917:284). The presence of quite a large number of Muslims in the region may be a sign of their dominance in historical times; in addition there is a greater concentration of the Marwaris, a business community. Culturally, Bharko is located in the region called Angdesh, where the ancient Vikram Shila University existed and consequently, the language which the people speak is known as Angika, which has affinity with Maithili.[2] Roy Chaudhury (1962:1). "North of the Ganges was Videha or Mithila, which was very early a great seat of Sanskrit learning, and included the modern Districts of Darbhanga, Champaran, and North Muzaffarpur; the south of the latter District continued the small kingdom of Vaishali! To the east lay Anga, including Monghyr, Bhagalpur and Purnea, as far as the Mahananda river. There are constant references to these countries in the Mahabharata."[3] (1909:18).

Historical Perspective

Bharko, the village under study, along with three more important villages — namely Rampur, Kumarpur and Gorigaon, is situated in an interior area — all falling under the jurisdiction of the police station — Amarpur in the Banka subdivision of the district of Bhagalpur. On the basis of a few historical records and accounts furnished by Hunter, Buchanan, K.K. Basu and others, it can be said that the entire region was governed by a Yadava named Chattur. Emperor Akbar granted these two tappas (a territorial division generally smaller in size than a Pargana but comprising more than one village) to Gurry Berm. But subsequently, this estate was divided between the two claimants — Munny Berm and Chattur Berm, the decendants of Gurry Berm — Barkope falling to the share of the former and Patsundah to the latter.[4] K.K. Basu (1932:111:112).

Again, the Persian Record No. 3(still kept intact with Sri Raghunandan Prasad Choudhary an old man of the village) and records of the zamindars of Bhagalpur substantiate Chattur's stronghold over the surrounding areas. "Jhajhur, the original Rajput proprietor of these tappas (Chandeep and Chanduarry) mortgaged these estates to a Hindu, by caste a Guwallah, and subsequently transferred them by sale to the latter in 1800 H (1599-1600 A.D.)"[5]. K.K. Basu (1932:113). The topographic description of the tappas is as under :—

"Tappa Chanduarry was about 12 miles from north to south and 8 miles from east to west at the time of permanent settlement in the year 1793. The boundary was —

East — Chandan river

West — Barna river

North — Kherahi Pargana and Bonamahill

South — Kojhi and Dhanre Sankhware."[6]

R.K. Chaudhury (1956:1)

Bharko and nine other villages together constituted Tappa Chanduarry.

Choudhary

Emperor Akbar made Chattur a Choudhary or the head-man — incharge of these tappas to collect revenue or maintain peace and order; and since then, his descendants retained the title. Francis Buchanan (1928:636:637) observed that the family title of the people of Chanduarry was Choudhary, i.e., the Chief of a village of an estate as the case may be. Even today 39 families of the Yadavas, out of a total of 105 families living in Bharko, call themselves as Choudhary, a title indicative of their possession of wealth or landed property, if not their descent from Chattur. These, and still some more accounts, go to prove that the Choudharies, by virtue of their valour and wealth, held supremacy over the areas for nearly four hundred years. That the area was under the control of the Choudharies is evident from the Collectorate Records of the 16th July, 1780. The Collector reported to Warren Hastings : "Since the dispossession of Raja Mozzafer Ali (1734:1773) ot Kharagpur, the country was under the Choudharies and Talugdaras, and in some places under Mondals and Mokaddamas". The Collector further recommended that the country, for the present, should remain under the management of the Choudharies.[7] R.K. Chaudhury (1956:2:3)

Sri Raghunandan Prasad Choudhary, on the basis of a comprehensive geneology, claims Chattur as his ancestor and affirms that his ancestors were zamindars right from the time of Akbar. Perhaps, this holds good even today as most of the Choudharies are big land-owners and, thereby, occupy a dominant position in the day-to-day affairs of the village. On revelation by Sri Choudhary and others of their origin from Shyamal, who is thought to be no other person than the Berman king, Muharajadhiraj Shyamal Bermadeo, whose father Jat Berman had conquered the ancient Angdesh; and, as the village is situated in Angdesh and is still regarded as an old village of Yadavas of Shyamal origin, it is just possible that Shyamal Bermadeo himself might have established it. Berngope, the original name of the village, had subsequently undergone several modifications — Bargo, Barko, Barkope and, ultimately Bharko. Beginning from Shyamal Bermadeo to the time of Chattur, the village had been the centre of administrative and military organization[8]. Dr. A.K. Chaudhury (Page-1) Dr. Raj Bali Pandey in his, "Jadu Bansh Ka Itihas' observes that the Bermans came from the Punjab and ruled in East Bengal in the second half of the 11th Century.

The Choudharies, who are said to have racial affinity with the Bermans, were very brave and victorious. They were also widely known for their religious temperament, particularly for their devotion to Lord Vishnu, and charity of land to the Brahmins. The descendants of Chattur Berm-Narayan and Dhana Ram; gave land measuring 1233 bighas and 5 kathas in charity to the Brahmins in the year 1759-60 for the worship of Vishnu in Mainma, a village in tappa Chandeepah. The gift document bore signatures of the givers and the seal of the registration office and is still available with Sri Chaudhary. According to him, under Chattur's care grew several villages within a radius of fifteen miles, marked by distinctiveness of language and culture of the Yadavas. A Brahmin was given seven bighas of land for performing worship and other occupational duties. The descendants of this particular Brahmin family are still in the village. Choudharine, the wife of Deem Chand Choudhary, was immensely devoted to religion and it is believed that she acted as convener of the association of religious preachers Brahmin widows in particular were guaranteed all help and protection. Temple priests and holymen from various religious places in the country used to be honoured and taken care of.

Notwithstanding these accounts, there are some more written records equally valuable, that explain the extent to which Chattur's descendants, being wealthy and powerful, were secured in privileged position in the State, beginning from the days of Akbar up to the first decade of the 19th Century.[9] (1966:14). There can be little doubt that the family enjoyed not only the rights of zamindari but also some judicial rights and it was incumbent on them to see to the preservation of peace in the area. In a Hukumnama, sealed by the Judge of Bhagalpur (dated 3rd July, 1917) it is stated that they were vested with judicial rights and were ordered to maintain peace and order in that region. They were asked to help the government in assessing the crime position and to find out ways and means for its prevention. This shows that till the first quarter of the

20th Century the family enjoyed sufficient statuts and position which they had acquired in the days of the Great Mughals.[10] R.K. Chaudhury (1956:9)

With the passage of time, things have changed enormously but the Choudharies still retain their superior position and dominate in the day-to-day affairs of the village. Apart from these historical accounts, even a few local sayings confirm the grant of landlordism to the Choudharies of this region by the Mughals. Indeed, it seems insignificant to refer to these sayings in view of the already established historical facts; however, one is quite interesting and illuminating because it reveals the attitude of love and compassion, religious sentiment and superstition prevalent among them and, as such, deserves to be mentioned.

Once a group of persons, mostly old men and women, were on a pilgrimage to certain holy places in the country. When night fell, all of them broke their journey in the village to resume it next morning. Meanwhile, a Brahmin widow in the team suffered seriously from cholera, making her condition alarmingly critical. Finding it quite difficult for them to stay on owing to her ailment, they all proceeded on, leaving her to the care of the people over there. The Choudharies, under whose care she was left, took all effective steps to save her life and, fortunately enough, the woman was cured. Having nobody in her family and knowing no other place where to seek shelter, she continued to remain in the village till her death.

As days rolled on, the woman began to be looked upon with awe by the villagers for her magical power. In every matter, from minor physical suffering to major social catastrophe, her advice was considered invaluable. Though it was not recognized in the beginning while she maintained herself by begging, yet subsequently an in-falliable belief in her supernatural power developed among the Choudharies. Just at an opportune moment, some members of the royal family happened to visit Amarpur, which is about six miles away from the village. Accidently, a woman in the family broke her leg from a fall resulting in the dislocation of her bone. Naturally, other members of the family were perturbed because it was not a question of acute and unbearable pain alone, but perphaps, a case of a woman in Purdah (veil) as well. When it seemed an uphill task for the specialists to set the bone in its proper place without having the sight and touch of the affected part, the wizard-widow was ultimately requested, and she readily agreed to treat her. As a part of the recipe, a horse with all its leg fastened tightly, was kept on fast for four days. The lady was asked to ride the horse on the fifth day, while someone whipped it twice and twice it jumped, and ultimately she was cured. All this happened in the presence of the inmates only, prohibiting observation by any outsider because of the Purdah system.

Being graciously pleased with the sense of duty and faithfulness to the Raja, the waiting Yadavas were asked to beg some help, if any, in return. Then they narrated their difficulty regarding non-availability of grazing land. There upon they were permitted to let loose all their cattle for full twenty-four hours and to report the distance which the animals covered within the scheduled time. They communicated twenty miles from north to south and eighteen miles from east to west (this being the area of the two tappas before permanent settlement) and land within the range was ordered to be theirs. Thus the Choudharies received ownership of land in the shape of Zamindari over the area as well as the Choudhary surname from the Mughals.

The content of the story, when carefully analysed leads not only to the establishment of a veritable correlation between the historical facts and the social saying but also portrays a deep inner religious attachment, a motely of beliefs and superstitions, a pattern of culture and structure of value of the Choudharies in a rural setting of this State.

Climate

The climate, except in rainy season, is considered suitable for the general physical health of the people. It is characterised by a hot summer and is followed by a cold, but pleasant, winter. The summer season starts from March and lasts till June. May is the hottest month with the average daily maximum temperature of 98.6° F and it may sometimes go upto 45° C (113° F) in the early part of June and before the outset of the south-west monsoon. Several cases of sunstroke are received in between May-June. Relief from the excessively dry and oppresive heat comes with the arrival of monsoon in July-August. The cold season starts in Novermber and lasts till February. January is the coldest month with the average maximum daily temperature of 74.5° F and the minimum of 45.5° F. During cold wave, which sometimes affects the people, temperature goes down to the freezing point.[11] P.C Roy Choudhury (1962:28).

The monsoon comes in July-August with a downpour, sometimes causing devastating floods. No doubt, the season has many odds, but to crown them all it brings the year's cherished hopes and aspirations of the farmers. The prospect of good crops directly depends on the rainfall and a failure of it means severest drought and famine, as is the case this year. The general agricultural activity, particularly paddy plantation, begins in this season.

The following table indicates the monthly variation in the rainfall* :—

TABLE NO. 1

Month	1961-62	1962-63	1963-64	1965-66
July	205.4 m.m.	213.7	106	323.1
August	272.1	306.6	173.8	313.6
September	158.1	179.4	121	398.2
October	191.4	110.4	246	10
November	...	...	...	...
December	...	...	...	...
January	...	...	2	...
February	...	...	...	...
March	...	...	...	...
April	...	16	39.2	...
May	45	104.4	17	0.18
June	129.3	123.4	120	47.5

*The figures in the above table were supplied by the Statistical Officer, Block Development Office, Amarpur, Bhagalpur,

Soil

The physical or natural environment that envelops the village is singularly marked by picturesque hills and forests, and mostly by the river, soil, climate and other resources. A series of barren rocks going up to Jamalpur, covered with green forests in which are occasionally seen tigers, provide spots for sight-seeing, picnic and game.

The soil is good and quite suitable for a variety of agricultural crops. There are mainly two types of soil—sandy and sandy-loam. J. Byrne (1911) mentions that 'sandy soil is known as Balmut that will grow anything whereas loamy soil is known as Doras on which, if low-lying, winter rice is grown but if high, various Bhadoi and Rabi crops do well.' The sandy soil is suitable for paddy, maize and tuber crops whereas sandy-loam is for paddy, wheat, barley, gram and other para crops.

Outside Communication

Bharko is connected with the world outside through numerous channels of communication. There are three bus routes from Bhagalpur to reach the village. Two routes remain open throughout the year but third one is closed during rainy season. The last one is the shortest, but, unmetalled on which only private buses ply, going straight to the village which is their terminus. Further, bullock carts and cycles are the other means of transportation to and from the village.

Quite a good number of people have gone to important towns and cities in the country, the well-to-do among them on pilgrimage and the poorer in search of jobs. A good number of the poor and landless labourers are absorbed at Bhagalpur and Calcutta on monthly or daily wages in various jobs. Among the important towns and cities which the people have so far visited are Bhagalpur, Deoghar, Gaya, Calcutta and Banaras. Through the operation of village exogamy, kinship ties and inter-village organization, Bharko maintains outside communication.

The People

The people of the village are compatible with those of the north Indian villages in respect of food, dress, customs, habits, agricultural operation, attitudes, beliefs as well as internal organization. The village exhibits unity and solidarity in times of natural catastrophe, calamity and enmity with other villagers. The presence of mutually organized council of elders consisting of influential persons is a great help to the villagers in resolving internal disputes before they are referred to the multi-village Panchayat. No doubt, the autonomy and self-sufficiency of the village have shattered still in certain internal matters, like patterns of settlement and mutual adjustment viewed in the context of wider organization, the same are believed to have been retained.

According to the census of 1961, Bharko, excluding two of its hamlets — Baja aud Souhua, has a total of 2308 inhabitants. During five years the number has come to 2608.

There are altogether 433 families living in the village represented by twenty two castes leaving aside an individual Marwari immigrant. The following is the number of families represented by the various castes :—

Yadava — 105,

Brahmin — 39,

Baniya — 9, Kamar — 3, Halwai — 3,

Kumhar — 11,

Lohar — 1,

Sonar — 2, Nai—12, Dhanuk—29, Gorhi—6,

Laheri — 1, Surhi — 50, Teli — 1, Beldar—23,

Julaha — 22, Dhobi—12, Chamar—61, Dusadh—6, Hari—2, Bengali Kayastha—1 and Kharadi—35. The following table indicates the population characteristics of the village :—

TABLE No. 2*

POPULATION DISTRIBUTION BY AGE, SEX & CASTE, 1961*

Age	*Yadava*		*Brahmin*		*Surhi*		*Dhanuk*		*Chamar*		*Muslim*		*Others*		*Total*	
	M	*F*	*M*	*F*	*M*	*F*	*M*	*F*	*M*	*F*	*M*	*F*	*M*	*F*	*M*	*F*
0-5	56	46	25	22	46	29	17	25	22	47	19	11	65	65	250	245
6-11	41	43	18	25	26	26	6	14	15	27	13	9	42	50	161	194
12-17	36	23	14	5	21	16	14	3	14	6	15	6	28	16	142	75
18-23	12	20	4	6	18	18	3	8	12	9	7	4	29	24	85	89
24-29	34	42	13	13	15	18	12	9	28	27	10	13	30	18	142	140
30-35	25	20	10	9	10	16	9	10	13	18	9	8	22	30	98	111
36-41	15	15	5	5	9	7	7	2	8	6	8	2	21	12	73	49
42-47	10	14	6	3	5	10	3	2	7	5	5	2	15	15	51	51
48-53	16	22	4	9	15	9	6	6	6	5	5	4	18	21	70	76
54-59	10	13	—	1	4	1	3	3	6	9	2	2	11	10	36	39

60-65	11	11	2	3	3	5	2	4	5	5	2	2	10	4	35	43
66-71	4	6	—	1	1	1	2	1	3	2	—	1	6	4	16	16
72-77	4	4	—	1	2	2	—	—	—	1	—	1	—	1	6	10
78—	—	3	—	—	—	—	—	1	—	3	4	—	—	3	4	10
Total :	274	282	101	103	175	158	84	88	139	170	99	65	297	273	1169	1139

*An up-to-date birth and death register kept with the Gram Sewak of the Panchayat office shows a total of 300 births and 165 deaths, i.e., an increase of 135 births or 5·8% rise in the total population of the Village during 1961-66.

The age distribution of the population is quite uneven. It is interesting to note that the males have outnumbered the females, the total number of males being 1169 and that of the females being 1139 in a total of 2308 people. The numerical strength of the Yadavas alone comes to 556 and that of the rest is as follows :—

Brahmin —204, Surhi —333, Chamar and Hari —309, Dhanuk —172, Muslims —164, and other 570.

The above Table shows the Yadavas as the strongest of all ; the second and third positions are occupied by the Surhis and Chamars respectively while the Brahmins are a little more than the Dhanuks and Muslims. The position of other castes in respect of number is negligible in the village.

The village presents a complex structure due to the presence of the Muslims whose religious culture is quite different from that of their Hindu counter-part. But for all practical purposes in the village they are assigned the status of a separate caste. A further classification of the people on the basis of religion may be made in the manner given in Table No. 3 given below :

TABLE 3.

POPULATION DISTRIBUTION BY RELIGION, 1961

Religion	*Number*	*Percentage*
1. *Hindus*		
(a) Clean Caste	1171	50.8
(b) Unclean or Backward caste	585	25.3
(c) Untouchable or Scheduled Caste	388	16.8
II *Muslim*	164	7.1
Total	2308	100%

The Village

The total area of the village is 3526.74 acres out of which the inhabitant area alone comes to 75.13 acres.*

Apparently the village ranks among the larger villages of the region with a number of dwellings quite close to each other. Bharko in a compact village and the reasons for its compactness, as reported by the inhabitants, are family partition, non-availability of land for housing purposes and fear of theft. These are quite prominent features of the region and they may not equally be obtainable in other parts of the state.

Bharko is situated on both sides of the unmetalled road which actually divides it into two distinct parts. The conventional ranking of caste has played a significant role in determining the pattern of habitation in the village. Each caste is located in separate tolas which are differentiated according to their castes. In fact, untouchability has been abolished in the country and its practice in any form is punishable, nevertheless it continues to exist.

As reported earlier, the private bus service from Bhagalpur to Bharko remains suspended during rainy season as the roads become muddy and except the government buses, private buses are not permitted to ply on the metalled roads. In such a situation or even when the bus develops any mechanical trouble, villagers are required either to walk some six miles or cover the distance by cycle or on bullock cart so as to get the bus at Amarpur. Buses arriving late stand in the village till night and leave only the next morning. All passengers including those from neighbouring areas, are supposed to get down at the village-market and walk to their destination. As there is nothing like passengers' waiting hall, people have to sit on the road-side or near a few tea and betal stalls lodged in huts which have sprung over there.

The village streets are quite narrow and dirty, making the movements of carts and pedestrians quite difficult. A peculiar

---

* Supplied by the village Karmachari incharge of Government records relating to land and revenue.

characteristic of the villagers is that, perhaps due to the fear of snakes and scorpions which abound the village, they urinate, at night on the streets in front of their houses. This sometimes makes movement quite impossible. Moreover, those, who are unable to provide cattle-shed for their animals and cattle, keep them on the road-side opposite their houses and this also contributes to the streets being dirty. But it is chiefly during rains that people experience great difficulty when the roads are muddy.

The village has a small post office housed in one room owned by a villager who runs a fair price shop and deals in medicines. Generally, ordinary mails are delivered to the people in the weekly market or sent through their co-villagers who happen to come to the post office for some personal work. There is no police station but a police outpost with only one constable. The police outpost lodged in a hut is situated near the market opposite a liquor shop. In view of mounting crime in the village and the area around, the government has ordered for an outpost in the village. Apart from this, the village has a health sub-centre under the care of a compounder and a trained midwife who reside in the village and attend emergency calls. Though the block medical officer is supposed to visit the centre at least twice in a week, particularly on the weekly market days, yet he comes only infrequently. It is only the Block Veterinary Doctor who visits the weekly market twice and examines the suffering animals and cattle in the market itself where they are brought in good number. The work of distributing medicine and offering treatment to the leprosy patients is performed by the mobile dispensary which is seen in the village on market days. There are altogether two unregistered allopaths, seven Ayurvaids, fourteen homeopaths and one Chandsi in the village.

A large-scale Government multipurpose co-operative society under the care of a manager adds to the new features of the village. The Society renders invaluable service to the peasants by advancing agricultural loans against surety of their agricultural produce. The society also sells fertilizers, manures, etc. among the farmers at cheap and controlled rates. In a large measure, these commendable steps of the Government have minimised the sufferings and anxieties of a number of poor peasants. Besides the co-operative manager, Government officials working at the village level include the Gram Sewak of the panchayat, the Karmachari, the village level worker, the compounder, midwife and the disinfector, all from the Block Development office at Amarpur.

The multi-village panchayat and the Kacherry are the other important scenes which the village provides. At the village level, the Panchayat is the highest executive body which undertakes to implement various rural reconstruction programmes. Criminal cases are looked into by the Mukhiya, the Chief Executive head, while judicial cases are referred to the Sarpanch who is incharge of the judiciary.

Lack of dexterity and hard work are the other traits exhibited by the village. It is not unusual to find several groups of people playing cards for hours together at different places in the village. Those who are not busy with cards are sitting either leisurely or spending their time in gossip. It is somewhat strenuous for an outsider to work in the village as quite a large number of people crowd near him almost everyday.

Women of higher castes observe purdah and are therefore not seen outside their houses except on certain ceremonial occasions. In that way they are unlike the women in Rampur who are invariably seen in files carrying water-loads as described by Lewis. Males are always in Dhoti and shirt whereas females are in Sari and blouse. Children, often seen playing indigenous games, are clad in half-pant and half-shirt.

The village has a regular market but, in certain respects, it is quite different from other village markets. To a casual observer it appears at first that probably the village has no market other than the weekly one because most of the shops remain closed for days together and open on the weekly market days only. Besides, many of them are located in the residential houses and are, therefore, not easily distinguished by an observer. The shopkeeper deals chiefly in grains that are kept in sacks inside the residential houses or, at best, in godowns. Hardly two or three grocery shops are kept open both in the morning and evening but customers do not crowd in these shops as generally they make purchases in the weekly market.

Outwardly, Bharko maintains friendly terms with the village in the neighbourhood and more so with its two hamlets that are directly dependent on it. But save and except these two settlements, all other surrounding villages are quite independent in their internal affairs. The Yadavas are the most powerful and influential in these villages and, in many respects, it is they who practically dominate the scene. Kinship and marriage ties, rites and ceremonies connected with caste, certain religious and cultural functions are the occasions when visits between the people of the village and those of its neighbourhood are exchanged. The inter-village organization helps as far as possible to promote mutual understanding among the people by resolving conflicts and disputes arising out of wrong demarcation of plots, use of canal water, benefit of irrigational facilities and other related matters. The Panchayat of the village exercises its influence even beyond Kolakashpur in the north, Kathara Shadpur in the west and Ram Chandra Etaṛhi in the east.

Housing

It is not so much the principal of super-ordination and subordination as the traditional caste hierarchy which has gone a long way in influencing village habitation. If viewed in this context, the village appears to have come into being according to some planning. The Choudharies and Brahmins form two separate blocks lying adjacent to the main thoroughfare which runs from east to west. The Surhis and Gorhis have built their houses to the north of the road encircling the entire area where the weekly market is held. It has to be stressed that the village is divided into various tolas which are called after the names of castes inhabiting them. A few furlong away from the main road in the north are the houses of the Muslims known as Kharadi. The Chamars, Haris and Dusadhs have built their houses at the eastern periphery of the village in different tolas. Likewise, the Dhobis and Kamars have erected their houses in the west, the Binds in the south, the Halwais and Baniyas in the north. Thus, there are almost as many tolas as there are castes in the village. No doubt, caste hierarchy did influence village habitation in the past but the same has become ineffective to-day except in the case of an untouchable caste.

The following indicates the categories or types of houses built in the village :—

(1) Pakka—made up of cement and bricks with R.C. Roof.

(2) Kachcha — Mudbuitt house with roofs covered with straw.

(3) Kachcha - Pakka—half brick-built and half mud-built.

(4) Pakka—madeup of cement and bricks but with tin or straw roofing.

(5) Hut — madeup of straw.

I. Ghar — residential houses.

II. Baithak — a long verandah with an attached room used by male members including visitors, guests and others. The room is also used for storing grain, wood, furniture etc.

III. Gohal — used as cattle-shed.

The village has the largest number of Kachcha houses. As the total number of pakka houses is only twenty eight and that of huts two, the rest of them, numbering 799, belong to the category of kachcha houses. Only those, who are economically and financially sound, can afford to live in pakka houses, but for those, who are poor, such houses are costly. Earlier, it has been mentioned that majority of the shops are located in the residential houses. The castewise distribution of such shops is thus : Brahmin—1, Surhi—33. Muslim—21, Sonar—1, Lohar—1, Baniya—6, Halwai—3, Gorhi-4 and Teli—1. There are two godowns; each belongs to a Yadava and a Surhi. The village has only one somewhat modern and impressive residential building which belongs to a Brahmin who is presently supposed to be the moneyed man of the village.

The distribution of houses in the village is quite uneven, at least from the standpoint that any one, whether of higher or lower caste, can live in any type of house anywhere in the village. The Choudharies are economically better off compared to the Brahmins and Surhis in the village, still many of them prefer to live in mudbuilt houses. Quite apart from those who have already constructed cemented houses, a few more among the Brahmins and Surhis can very well afford to construct similar houses. According to the villagers, Pakka houses generally indicate their owners' state of richness and as such extend invitation to dacoits and thieves. Hence the factor which, largely prevents them from constructing these houses is the fear of dacoits and thieves. Inwardly they cannot be gratiflied with living in mudbuilt houses but they are helpless. These people are conscious that Kachcha houses, beside being shapeless or formless, are quite uncomfortable and unhealthy. Such houses neither have proper ventilation nor sufficient accomodation and light. Moreover, they are socially discreditable, even then they can't altogetehr be discarded. For the poor either mudbuilt houses or huts are the must.

Education

Education has its unique and unparalleled significance for individuals in a community, whether rural or urban. Professor Humayun Kabir expresses his views on education — "Since man cannot live by himself, the aim of all systems of education whether of East or West, is to help individuals become better members of their community. Education today has become all the more important for all nations, particularly for those that are underdeveloped. In India it is spreading by leaps and bounds even among rural communities."[12] Humayun Kabir (1955 : 101).

According to the Census of 1961, the total number of literate males and females in the entire Mouje, having a total of 6085 people, respectively, is 868 or 28.5% and 207 or 6.5%. Besides, the percentage of literates is 17.6 and that of illiterates 82.4. Although the number of illiterates is larger than that of the literates, yet the tempo at which education is spreading in the village clearly indicates that, by and by, the literates will outnumber the illiterates. People have now become quite enthusiastic about the education of their children which is proved by the rise in the number of schools and school attendance. In the past the village had only one primary or vernacular school for the infants. Later on a Government Middle School came into existence which, subsequently, gave impetus for the establisment of a high school. Only the Choudharies are accredited with making financial contribution and giving unstinted co-operation in regard to the establishment of a high school in the village. As the Brahmins are jealous of the educational advancement of the Yadavas, they indirectly endeavour to foil any effort made by the latter, as others are not at all concerned for the educational progress of the villagers. However, after a good deal of efforts they have succeeded in getting government's recognition for the High School upto the Xth Class. Details of the types of schools, number of teachers etc. are given in the following tables :—

TABLE No. 4

TYPE AND NUMBER OF SCHOOLS IN BHARKO.

Type of School	*Number*
1. Lower Primary School	1
2. Middle School	1
3. High School	1
4. Madarsa for Muslim infants	1
Total	4

TABLE No. 5

NUMBER OF TEACHERS IN SCHOOLS

School	*Number*		*Total*
	M.	*F.*	
Lower Primary School	1	2	3
High School	6	x	6
Middle School	4	x	4
Madarsa	1	x	1
Total	12	2	14

The gradual increase in the number of schools and teachers in the village reflects people's favourable attitude towards education. This is also proved by the fact that, as compared to past years, the number of students has slightly increaed (2.5%) in the recent time. Quite a good number of boys and girls receive education in these schools. As there is no separate school for girls, these schools have co-education right from the elementary up to the secondary stage. Introduction of co-education, in fact, indicates restlessness of the villagers for the causes of female education as well as a new direction towards social change. The standard of teaching in the elementary school is not up to the mark; as a consequence pupils are also sent to the so-called village school masters for receiving lessons. An outsider is much impressed to find these pupils, other than those in the elementary school, cheerfully sitting in open places in the village and taking lesson from their masters.

Primary education, which is of basic type, is free and compulsory but the response is quite meagre. School attendance with regard to age, sex and caste is shown in the table on the next page.

These figures do not seem to be encouraging. However, when compared to the position of education in the past, they are definitely satisfactory except that the progress is slow. More-

TABLE No. 6

SCHOOL ATTENDANCE WITH REGARD TO AGE, SEX AND CASTE

Age	*Yadava*		*Brahmin*		*Surhi*		*Baniya*		*Kamar*		*Teli*		*Chamar*		*Kumhar*		*Nai*		*Beldar*		*Julaha*		*Muslim*		*Gorhi*		*Total*	
	M.	*F.*	*F.*	*M.*	*M*	*F.*	*M.*	*F.*	*M.*	*F.*	*M.*	*F.*	*M.*	*F.*	*M.*	*F.*	*M.*	*F.*	*M.*	*F.*	*M.*	*F.*	*M.*	*F.*	*M.*	*F.*	*M.*	*F.*
0-5	—	—	—	—	—	—	—	—	—	—	—	—	—	—	—	—	—	—	—	—	—	—	7	5	—	—	7	5
6-11	28	14	14	19	21	14	2	3	1	—	1	—	9	—	2	—	2	—	8	—	5	—	8	7	—	—	7	5
12-17	70	21	18	8	19	4	4	—	—	—	2	—	12	—	1	—	2	—	—	—	1	—	1	—	1	1	103	58
Total	98	35	33	27	40	18	6	3	1	—	3	—	21	—	3	—	4	—	8	—	6	—	16	12	2	2	241	96

over, in the above table the Yadavas are at the top and then come successively the Surhis and the Brahmins while education among other castes mentioned in the table is almost negligible.

A few castes like Lohar, Halwai, Dhobi, Sonar, Hari etc; whose children have no schooling at all, are not included in the above table. No doubt, there are a few graduates among the Yadavas and Brahmins and some are prosecuting their studies in the University, but they are quite nominal.

REFERENCES

CHAPTER II

1. O'Mallay, 1917, *Bengal, Bihar and Orissa, Sikkim.* (University Press, Cambridge).

2. Roy Chaudhury, P.C., 1962, *Bihar District Gazetters* (*Bhagalpur*), (Superintendent, Secretariat Press, Bihar, Patna).

3. *Imperial Gazeteer of India* (*Bengal*), Volume—I, 1919, (Superintendent of Government Printing, Calcutta).

4. Basu, K.K., 1932, *The Zamindars of Bhagalpur—Bengal* : *Past And Present*, Volume XLIII, Pt. II, No. 86.

5. Basu, K.K., 1932

6. Chaudhury, R.K., 1956, *History of Tappa Chanduarry, Tappa Chandeepah* (Journal of the Bihar Research Society, Vol. XLII, Pt. 3-4 Reprint).

7. *Ibid*

8. Chaudhury, *A.K.*, *Yadavo Ka Berman Rajkul*, Hindi Manuscript, Unpublished.

9. Yadava' in Hn., 1966, Daranagar, Varanasi, Pt. 5.

10. *Ibid.*

11, *Ibid.*

12. Kabir, H., 1955, *Science, Democracy And Islam And Other Essays* (George Allen & Unwin Ltd., Ruskin House, Museum St., London).

CHAPTER III

Caste Structure

Nature of Caste

Caste, a significant unit of social structure, performs many important functions in the organization of the village. About the nature of caste, Hutton (1963:2) writes — "Each caste is a social unit in itself. The customs by which it lives are generally different in some respects from those of other castes, and are sometimes in marked contrast to those of any other caste at all. Persons of one caste do not marry those of another. The extent to which persons of one caste will eat or drink with those of another is strictly limited by unwritten laws and everybody knows who is affected by them. Even a change of religion does not destroy the caste system ..."[1] Caste is a basic and fundamental factor in the stratification of Hindu society. Writing on the social structure of Hinduism, Pannikar (1961:29) observes — "The structure revolves round two fundamental institutions, the caste and the joint family. Everything connected with the Hindu people outside their religion, is related to these two institutions. These in fact are the differentiating characteristics of Hindu life."[2] The four-fold division — Brahmin, Kshatriya, Vaishya and Shudra, are widely known to the people of India. This division of the Indian society was based on varna which was modified with the passage of time when the society headed towards greater complexity. Today, each family belongs to an exogamous division of caste based on lineage or Gotra, and several such divisions compose one endogamous caste or its section within a larger caste. Each caste has been assigned a particular calling, status, culture, tradition reinforced by religion. Restrictions on commensality inter-marrige etc. are imposed by the caste on its members which they are supposed to obey for fear of excommunication. Thus, caste exercises stringent control and regulates behaviour of the members in a community.

Caste and Occupation

Bharko represents 22 castes, each having an endogamous character and functioning independently of other castes; each caste has taken to a separate occupation although castes today are no longer identified by their traditionally assigned occupation. However, the various castes in the village, along with their population and conventional occupations, are shown in the table given below :

TABLE No. 1

DISTRIBUTION OF CASTE WITH REGARD TO POPULATION AND TRADITIONAL OCCUPATION.

Sl. No.	*Caste*	*Population*	*Percentage*	*Traditional Occupation*
1	2	3	4	5
1.	Yadava	556	24	Cattle-keepers or Milkmen
2.	Brahmin	204	8.8	Priests.
3.	Baniya	62	2.7	Traders.
4.	Kamar	28	1.2	Carpenters.
5.	Halwai	28	1.2	Confectioners.
6.	Kumhar	47	2.0	Potters.
7.	Lohar	1	0.04	Blacksmiths.
8.	Sonar	9	0.3	Goldsmiths.
9.	Nai	44	1.9	Barbers.
10.	Dhanuk	172	7.5	Service Men.
11.	Gorhi	24	1.0	Fishermen.

1	2	3	4	5
12.	Laheri	12	0.5	Bangle Makers.
13.	Surhi	333	14.5	Traders.
14.	Teli	8	0.3	Oil Pressers or Oilmen.
15.	Beldar	134	5.8	Labourers
16.	Julaha	100	4.3	Weavers,
17.	Dhobi	37	1.6	Washermen.
18.	Chamar	309	13.4	Shoemakers.
19.	Dusadh	20	0.8	Village Watchmen.
20.	Hari	9	0.4	Scavengers.
21.	Bengali — Kayastha	7	0.3	Betel Sellers
22.	Kharadi	164	7.2	Cotton Carders & Toy-makers.
	Total :—	2308	100	

In addition to the castes mentioned in the last table, there is one sectarian caste known as Bhat Brahmin, "a tawdry parody of the bard and genealogist of heroic times, whose rapacity and shamelessness are proverbial."[3] Sir Herbert Risley (1908:113). Their strength is only nine and I have included them, for convenience, in the population of the Brahmins, though the former is socially much inferior to the latter. They are non-priestly caste, maintaining themselves by reciting poems and telling stories from holy books to please the people and at the same time wandering from place to place or door to door for alms. The Kharadis are the Muslims who have specialized in toy making and cotton combing. There is nothing traditional with the peasant caste, as those who own land naturally belong to the caste of peasants, whereas those who do not, are obviously placed in the category of labourers. But, of course, the Brahmins, and for that reason the upper castes, do not want to be addressed as agriculturists, even if agriculture be their main occupation, as the said occupation carries less prestige outside the village.

Caste Divisions

Each caste is divided into various sub-castes or small groups of caste having special names by which they are known. These are all endogamous divisions which regulate marriage and interdining. Ketkar opines in this regard — "These divisions and sub-divisions are introduced on different principles. In this way two hundred million Hindus are so much divided and sub-divided that there arc castes which can not marry outside fifteen families."[4] Hutton (1963:48). Further, in his definition of caste, Mees mentions these divisons in this manner — "A society subjected to a caste system consists of a number of sub-divisions or castes which are exclusively endogamous, which show a strong tendency to be socially exclusive, which perpetuate themselves hereditarily, which are hierarchically supposed on a basis of standard supposedly cultural, and which by the working of these four tendencies within the social field of their own delimitations may split up into more and more castes indefinitely."[5] C.O. Cox (1959:5).

The following indicates the number of divisions among various castes in Bharko :—

Brahim—8, Yadava—6, Surhi—3, Beldar—6. Julaha—5, Teli—5, Dhobi—5, Dusadh—3, Kamar—4, Baniya—4, Chamar—6, Dhanuk—5, Kumhar—5, Laheri—4, Gorhi—5, Hari—5, Halwai—1, Sonar—2, Lohar—1, and Muslims—8.

But all these divisions are not found in the village. A brief description of those found in the village is as follows :—

Yadavas

According to Hutton, this caste combines within itself a few similar castes. He (1963:50:51) mentions — "One of the difficulties in defending caste is caused by a certain fluidity which shows itself most often perhaps in fissiparous tendencies, but sometimes of recent years in a tendency towards the amalgamation of analogous castes with a view to the exercise of social and political influence. Thus in 1931 there was a widespread movement on the part of various cattle-keeping castes — Ahirs, Aharas, Goalas, Gollas, Gopas, Idaiyans, etc. to combine under a new caste named as Yadava, though how far, if at all, such a movement would involve reciprocity in the matter of marriage is uncertain."[6] The Yadavas have two main divisions of which each one is endogamous. The Manjhraut and Dahiyar function independently in the matter of marriage and in respect of ceremonial feast. The Choudharies are the original settlers of the village, while others of the same caste are Bhaginmans (families of son-in-laws) who were given land by the Choudharies to settle in the village. Earlier, it has been stressed that the social position of the Choudharies is superior to that of the Brahmins as the former were the Maliks or Zamindars in the village and in the neighbouring areas. As in other castes, marriage outside the clan is prohibitory among all the Yadavas. In respect of interdining they are governed by clearly defined chattis consisting of families up to five or seven generations. In all there are four such chattis among the Choudharies, one among the Mahtos and the rest among others. As members of the caste happen to be kin they do not intermarry in the village.

Baniyas

Out of the four divisions, only two are found in the village. The Vaishya Baniya is superior to the Agrahi Baniya because the latter practises widow marrige. Both are endogamous in character and both observe restrictions on commensality or interdining and differ even in their occupations. The first deals in groceries whereas the second in herbs, roots and indigenous medicines, though both of them are agriculturists and shopkeepers in the village.

Surhis

Out of the three divisions two are present in the village. The Saundic group considers itself superior to the other group because the latter sells wine, although both the groups are not endogamous. The entire caste is regarded as unlean in the sense that people do not accept water from their hands.

Beldars

They have six divisions but none of them, except the whole caste is endogamous. Hence, restrictions on intermarriage and interdining are not observed by them. These Beldars are fishermen and labourers. They are expert at cutting soil for agricultural purposes and wood for fuel in the village.

Julahas

Out of five divisions, two are found in the village. One group has Sanskritized itself by calling itself as Tantu Vaishya. This group pursues weaving as its main occupation and, thereby, regards itself as superior in culture, custom and occupation to the other group. Both the groups are endogamous and maintain social difference in respect of marriage and interdining between them.

Mulsims

Out of eight, only one division, which is an endogamous one, is found in the village. The people of this group are cotton carders (Dhuniyas) and toy-makers (Kharadi) or are otherwise artisans.

Telis

They are oil-pressers or oil-sellers. Out of their five divisions, only three are found in the village. These are not endogamous divisions, hence restrictions on intermarriage and interdining between them are not observed, though the caste as bigger group, is, no doubt, endogamous.

Dhobis

Out of five, only two divisions are present in the village. Both are endogamous and socially independent of each other. Distinctiveness in the matter of marriage and interdining is strictly observed by each of the group. Members of both the groups are Hindus and are the washermen of the village.

Dusadhs

All the three divisions are found in the village. Each of the three divisions is endogamous in character and is distinct in many respects like commensality or interdining. They are the village watchmen, but most of them are absorbed as agricultural labourers. They belong to the group of Domes (Sweepers) taming swine and carrying dead animals out of the village. Of all the untouchable castes, this caste is despised most.

Dhanuks

Out of five, only two divisions are present in the village. They do not maintain their endogamous character, hence marriage and interdining between them are allowed. They are servant caste. In the marriage of a Choudhary's or Brahmin's daughter a female member of a Dhanuk caste accompanies the bride to her father-in-law's house as her maid servant. In the past, the male members used to carry palanquines in marriages but today carry on their shoulders only presents of their masters to the latter's relatives and friends. A few members of this caste, who are now somewhat economically better off, do not want their caste-men to do this job as it is somewhat disgraceful in nature. But the poor have no other way except to do it stealthily as, if observed, they may receive ex-communication from their caste.

Kumhars

All the five groups remain in the village. Three of them are endagamous but none of them observes restriction on interdining. Kumhar is a Jajmani caste and traditional occupation of its members is to supply earthen pots to their patrons on ceremonial occasions.

Chamars

Out of six divisions, three are found in the village. All these three are endogamous in nature, hence they strictly observe restrictions on marriage and interdining. Chamars are labourers in the field and, except two families, which are still following their traditional occupation of leather work, others have turned into agricultural labourers in the village.

Kamars

Of the four divisions, three are found in the village, but all of them are not at all endogamous. Therefore, marriage among these divisions is possible and there is no restrication on interdining. They are carpenters and they prepare plough, chairs and wooden doors in addition to cots and beds for the villagers.

Laheris

Out of four divisions, two are present in the village and, like Kamars, these two divisions do not maintain distance either in the matter of inter-group marriage or interdining. They prepare bangles for the women folk and that is their main occupation in the village.

Gorhis

Out of five divisions, only two are present but these two are absolutely endogamous, although they permit interdining. They are expert at catching fish and it is they who are the real fishermen. They are running a Fishermen's Cooperative Society for the development of pisci-culture. Besides one group prepares flowers, festoons, hats borne by the bride-grooms at the time of marriage, all made of paper. They decorate with flowers, garlands, festoons, leaves etc. the doors and places in their patron's house where marriage is to be celebrated.

Haris

Out of five groups, two are found in the village and both the two divisions are endogamous and do not allow either inter-group marriage or interdining. They are the sweepers of the village. When a child is born in a family, the female members of this caste would be sent for to act as untrained midwives or village chamains.

Halwais

Out of four divisions, only one is found in the village. According to a few informants of this caste, all these four are endogamous divisions but they don't have restriction on interdining. These people run small confectioneries in the village.

Sonars

Out of the two divisions, only one is found in the village. However, both allow inter-group marriage and interdining.

They are the goldsmiths of the village who live by preparing and selling ornaments.

Caste Hierarchy

Commonly, difficulty is experienced in arranging the various castes according to their hierarchy. Some of the informants though belong to the lower castes, to-day do not want to be classed as lower and, for that reason, do not regard their occupation as low, compared to the occupations of other castes of the same group. For instance, a blacksmith is not prepared to consider his caste or occupation as inferior to that of a carpenter. Though both the castes belong to the category of lower caste, in actual practice, the former is much inferior to the latter. In this complex situation, I would adopt the traditionally ascribed or hereditary status as the sound principle of caste hierarchy. At one stage of this issue Dr. Majumdar (1958:19) comprehends — "In the caste-culture configuration, entry into a social status is a function of heredity : individual achievement, personal quality or wealth have, according to the strict traditional prescription, no say in determining the social status. But an important point that now catches a social scientist's eye in the field of investigation is the growing discrepancy between theory and practice."[7] Hence, my adoption of the traditional basis of caste superiority is immediately fraught with the serious danger in arranging all the castes in Bharko according to the Varna system. The only course left now is to depend on the field data which help me to visualise the relative superiority of each caste in a hierarchical order.

This hierarchy among the various castes in the village is based not on a single factor rather on multiple factors—endogamy, commensality, occupation, diet, pollution etc. Professor Srinivas (1955:19) explains — "The essence of hierarchy is the absence of equality among the units which form the whole : in this sense, the various castes in Rampura do form a hierarchy. The caste units are separated by endogamy and commensality and they are associated with ranked differences of dietary and occupation."[8] Likewise, the various castes in Bharko are unequal in their status or position and even in their day-to-day relations they maintain a certain degree of social distance.

Besides, the existence of broad categories, numbering three, made on the basis of acceptance of food and water as well as observance of pollution itself leads to the admission of inequality among various castes in the village and elsewhere. According to these categories, the hierarchical arrangement of different castes in Bharko is described in the table given below :

Table No. 2

CASTE CATEGORIES WITH REGARD TO ACCEPTANCE OF FOOD AND WATER AND OBSERVANCE OF POLLUTION.

Category	*Caste*
1. Clean Caste	Brahmin, Yadava, Baniya, Kamar, Halwai, Kumhar, Lohar Sonar, Nai, Dhanuk, Gorhi, Laheri, Rarhi-Kayastha.
2. Unclean Caste	Surhi, Teli, Beldar, Julaha.
3. Untouchable Caste	Dhobi, Kharadi, Chamar, Dusadh, Hari.

As stated earlier, endogamy, commensality, occupation, diet and pollution are the significant bases which separate one caste from the other and rank it as superior or inferior. But this approach to a study of caste hierarchy is also not free from obscurity, as complete separation of caste, except in the matter of endogamy, is not objectively made particularly when caste restrictions on food and drink, commensality, untouchability etc. are not rigidly followed. Hence, it is possible to present only a tentative, but not a final, picture of statuswise groupings of castes.

Table No. 3

HIERARCHICAL GROUPING AMONG VARIOUS CASTES AT BHARKO.

Rank	*Caste*	
A	Brahmin	Bhat Brahmin (a Sectarian Caste)

B	Yadava, Baniya, Halwai, Surhi, Kamar, Lohar, Kumhar, Sonar, Nai, Laheri, Gorhi, Dhanuk, Teli, Beldar, Julaha, Kharadi.	Rarhi (Bengali) Kayastha.
C	Dhobi Dusadh	Chamar Hari,

The Brahmin is at the top tier of the caste hierarchy because tradition assigns it a preeminent position. "The preeminent and fixed position of the Brahmin in the hierarchy represents a fixed point in terms of which the ritual positions of other castes can be judged. Thus, a caste nearer the Brahmin on the hierarchy is in general more Brahminical and, therefore, its ritual status is higher than that of castes which are distant from the Brahmin and relatively less Brahminical."[9] K. S. Mathur (1964 : 123). It is not so much the nearness or the ritual status that matters most in caste hierarchy but the day-to-day social contacts or dealings between the castes which are important. For instance, in the general traditional ramification of caste, the Surhi is assigned a lower status and, as such, no Brahmin can accept food and water touched by a Surhi, but in day-to-day contacts or dealings the Surhis are given a superior position next to the Brahmins, the Yadavas being strategically superior to all.

Endogamy puts serious limitations on caste hierarchy and thereby, severely restricts the status positions of different castes in a community. Villagers regard marriage as a sacrament and, therefore, celebrate it within their own castes. Hence marriage of a Brahmin with a Dhobi or Chamar is considered as sacrilegious. Any surreptitious indulgence in a sexual act between them is a denial of Dharma. Thus, endogamy keeps apart one caste from the other. Similarly, commensality bifurcates the clean caste from the unclean and untouchable castes. A Brahmin does not accept food and water from the hands of a Surhi or a

Teli because they are considered as unclean castes. Again, possibility of social interaction and daily contact of a Brahmin with a Dusadh or Hari is negatively true for the latter are untouchables. The stereotyped notion about a Dusadh prevailing in the village is that one should talk to him at least from a distance of one and half yards or even beyond. Thus fear of pollution strengthens social distance among various castes in the village.

Occupational difference constitutes an important aspect of caste hierarchy. Certain occupations are considered very low. For example, the occupations of a shoemaker, scavenger and washerman are taken as low; of course, begging, stealing and prostitution are accepted as heinous occupations. A Chamar works in leather which is a defiling object. A washerman cleans dirty clothes including menstrual clothes. A Dusadh carries the carcase of a dead animal. The Hari and the Dusadh eat the flesh of goat, sheep, calf and pig and sell in the market the skin of dead animals and cattle. These are all mean and sordid occupations, hence the caste-Hindus despise them for being contrary to religion. Vegetarian food marks a caste as higher whereas non-vegetarian food marks it as lower. Drinking wine or taking intoxicating things is the sign of a lower caste. The Brahmin is held as superior to all the castes for taking vegetarian food and remaining aloof from alcoholic drinks. Except the Maithil Brahmins in the village and elsewhere the State, who are worshippers of Goddess Durga or Bhagawati, are therefore non-vegetarian, no other Brahmin eats mutton or fish. Of course these Maithil Brahmins in the village do not take eggs or chicken.

The traditional caste superiority of the Brahmins over all other castes is known to the Hindus. But except their caste superiority, in all other respects it is the Yadavas who are superior to all, including the Brahmins in the village, by virtue of their being the landlords and big cultivators. The Brahmins were the raiyats (tenants) of the Choudharies and were receiving all help and patronage from them. The Choudharies are still addressed as Maliks (Lords or Masters) by the people who are supposed to rise in their seats whenever a Choudhary happens to pass through the street in the village.

Inter-Caste Relations

The problem of inter-caste relations can meticulously be studied from two standpoints—

(a) Jajmani relations among different castes; and

(b) Relations among various other castes.

As regards Jajmani relations among different castes, one has to encounter the difficulty of particularising one caste as serving other castes when castes, at least in urban areas, are now no longer identified by their traditional occupations. However, in the village some remnants of the system are still to be seen among Brahmins, Nai, Kamar, Gorhi, Kumhar, Dhanuk, Dhobi, Chamar and Hari. These castes serve others for which they receive payments either in cash or in kind and are thus being served by them. Except the clean castes and also a few of the unclean castes which are rich, generally families of the unclean and untouchable castes do not engage any Jajman caste on ceremonial occasions but manage the affairs among themselves. Moreover, the question whether a Brahmin would like to preside over certain ceremonial occasions like birth, marriage and funeral in the families of the Chamar, Hari and Dusadh and whether a Nai would undertake to shave their heads and beard or render them other necessary services is also there. It has to be admitted that Jajmani system is gradually breaking away for which a number of factors are responsible. In the first place, and perhaps this has been the chief factor, members of these castes feel that continuance in their Jajmani professions is not profitable. Previously, members of the castes used to support their families with the incomes which they earned from these services. But, today, no family can depend on this profession for its maintenance. In the second place, chances of getting other suitable and more profitable employments have now increased within and without the village. One Nai is working as a Gram Sewak in the Office of the Village Panchayat. Except four families, which are still continuing their traditional occupation, all other families of the Chamars are absorbed in the village as agricultural labourers. A few Dhobis are working in Bhagalpur and other places as paid employees in laundaries and dryhouses. The Kamars and Kumhars sell their goods in the weekly market on ready cash. A few of them are working as labourers in the mills and factories at Calcutta.

Lastly, an increase in occupational mobility has led to the decline of the Jajmani system. These castes, which sustained in the past on their traditionally assigned occupations, are now switching over to other occupations because these occupations happen to be both profitable and prestigious. A Dhanuk feels embarrassed if he is required to do the job of a domestic servant. Hence, all of them have taken to other occupations. Lately, Jajmani system has received a severe jolt on account of a flexibility or fluidity, caused by modern science and technology, in the attitude of the people towards religious observances and practices. Besides, the possibilty of hard economic pressure of the people in the modern age serving as a factor in the break up of the system is already there. Consequently the Jajmani castes don ot entirely depend on their traditional occupation for their maintenance or livelihood and take to other jobs.

The following diagram illustrates the pattern of inter-castes relations between a Yadava and their nine Jajmani castes.

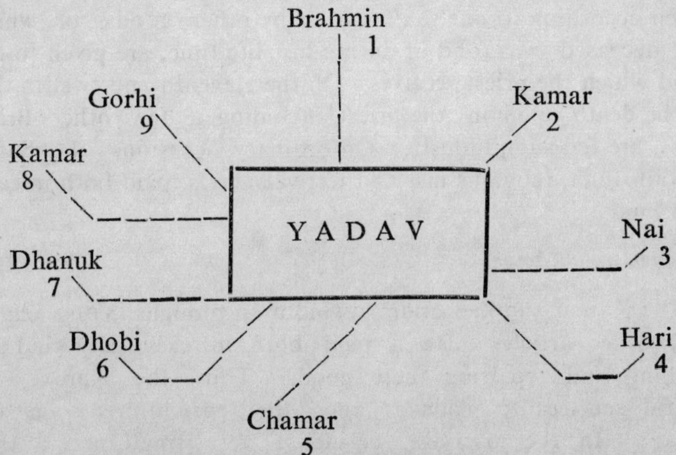

Sociogram showing Jajmani Relationship.

Service Rendered and Payment Received

Whenever an occasion comes in Yadava family that the services of a Brahmin are required, the latter readily agrees to render such services. When a child is born, the family priest is sent for. He consults his almanac and, examining the planetary position, foretells the fortune of the child. In return, some money and grain are paid to him. If a female child is born, the payment is less, but if it is the birth of of the first son, the Brahmin is paid handsomely. Similarly, the mode of payment varies in the marriage of a son or a daughter. In the marriage of a son, the Choudharies receive dowry; in their daughter's marriage, as most of the people do, they have to pay it. Hence, marriage of a son is profitable whereas that of a daughter is an investment without any return. Therefore, the rate of payment to a Brahmin varies. Usually, in a son's marriage he is paid one pair of Dhoti, a sum of Rs. 5/-, two days' meal and some grain, but in a daughter's marriage he is given one pair of Dhoti, a sum of Rs. 2/-, meals for both the days and a little grain.

On funeral occasions, the Brahmin is not given any clothes except what he receives as Dan (gift) which is believed to have been given to the deceased. Hence, in addition to clothes, utensils, cots and beds, cow, some immovable property, etc. given according to one's status, many other goods, of which the deceased was fond of during his life time, are given to the dead which the priest receives. On the eleventh and twelfth day of the death ceremony the priest, including a few other Brahmins, are fed sumptuously. On ordinary occasions like Satya Narain Puja, religious fast and festivals, he is paid both in cash and kind.

Yadava and Kamar

The Kamar supplies doors, windows, ploughs, cots, chairs and other articles. He is paid both in cash and kind for making and repairing these goods. Thus, the Kamar does useful services to Yadavas and other agriculturists in the village. In the marriage, besides a very small piece of thin wooden plank to be used in the Mandap, the place of marriage, a Kamar also supplies Pidha (wooden seats) for the bridegroom, bride and their parents.

Yadava and Nai

The number of occasions on which a Nai renders services to a Yadava or any other caste equals that on which a Brahmin renders services. In the village, a Nai serves a Yadava on the occasions of birth, marriage, death and other religious and ritual occasions. On the birth of a child, a male member of the caste shaves the beard and cuts the nails of the male members of his Jajman family, whereas a female member of the caste cuts the nails of the mother, of other females, as well as those of near kin on the purificatory day. On the sixth day known as Chhatti, the female Nai has to make all arrangements for the Puja and is paid a Sari, if it is the birth of a first male child, otherwise she is given some grain and food only on that day.

In the marriage, both the male and female members of the caste render necessary services. For four days after the marriage, the female member has to polish with cowdung the floor of the Mandap for the remaining ritualistic and customary observances. It is she who brings the bride from inside the house to the Mandap duriug marriage, while members of the marriage party, guests, invitees and other relations remain present to witness the marriage ceremony. Throughout, in the marriage of a daughter, the services of a female member of the caste are required. In the marriage of a son, the services of a male member of the caste are needed, right from betrothal upto the actual marriage ceremony. For a feast to be given to the castemen, a Nai has to give invitation, on behalf of the host, to the people and to call them when preparations get ready. He is paid a piece of Dhoti, money and grain. He gets only a little than what the Brahmin gets.

Yadav and Hari

It is the Hari woman who serves as a midwife at the time of delivery. She cuts the navel cord of the child and besmears mustard oil in the body both of the mother and the child for three days. Washing of dirty clothes, which she ultimately gets, till the period of Chhatti when both the mother and the child take purificatory bath, forms a part of her duty. She is given grain for her services prior and after delivery. On the Chhatti day she is fed sumptuously. Sweeping the area around the house is her routine job.

Yadava and Chamar

The Chamars till the agricultural land of the Yadavas for which they are paid a sum of Rs. 500/- as loan and are given land measuring five katthas for their maintenance. In return, they work for any number of plough needed by the Yadavas for agricultural operation. Both the loan money and the land are returnable in the event of failure to undertake the work.

Yadava and Dhobi :

The relationship between a Yadava and a Dhobi exists to the extent to which the latter is serviceable to the former. A Dhobi has to wash any number of dirty clothes given to him. He is paid in grain and, if necessary, in cash also on yearly basis. Besides, in the harvest season he is permitted to take a bundle of as much paddy, wheat and fodder as he can carry at a time. This applies not only to him but to all the Jajmani castes in the village.

Yadava and Dhanuk

Dhanuks are generally absorbed as domestic servants by the Choudharies. Besides, male members of this caste are asked to take presents from their masters to deliver them to their relations and kin who are living outside the village. In the daughter's marriage, a female member goes with the bride to her father-in-law's house as her maid servant and again comes back with her. In return for these services, besides clothes, money and some ornaments which she receives at both the places, the male members of the caste are given land on Bataidari (share-cropper) basis and are absorbed as tenants.

Yadava and Kumhar

The Kumhars supply earthen pots on ceremonial occasions of of Satya Narain Puja, they have to supply earthen plates for distribution of Prasad (food offered to the deity) and Diya (earthen lamps) to be offered to the deity. In marriage, they supply Kalasha (water pots or vessels), plates, lamps, elephants, all made up of clay, for being kept in the Mandap. On Deepawali festival, they supply earthen lamps and, for the children, Kulhia-Chukia (plaything). The mode of payment of all these is both cash and kind plus meals on the festival day.

Yadava and Gorhi

The Gorhis prepare Mauri (Crown) borne by a bridegroom at the time of marriage. On such an occasion, they decorate the doors, gates and the Mandap with flowers and festoons. On usual Puja days they supply flowers, Belpatras (leaves of Bel tree) and garlands to be offered to the deity. Besides, they make crackers which the people buy in large quantity especially for their use in marriage and Dewali festivals.

The relations between the Yadava and other castes are characterised by mutual co-operation as well as understanding of unity and solidarity. This can be learnt from a close study of the behaviours of each caste separately.

Yadava and Lohar

In the village there is only one Lohar having no other member in his family. He is serviceable to all castes including the Yadavas as he prepares agricultural implements which include Khurpa, Kudal, Hasuli, Hasua and plough-blades. He sharpens the scissor and razor of a Nai and repairs agricultural implements. The Yadavas utilise his services for agricultural purposes, too.

Yadava and Beldar

All the Beldars are agricultural workers. They are expert at levelling the agricultural field, digging soil and cutting woods for fuel. The swiftness and ease with which their small children can dig the soil and cut the woods will not be performed by adult members of other castes. The Yadavas engage adult members of this caste for agricultural work on daily wages.

Yadava and Julaha

Most of the members of this caste work as landless labourers in agricultural operations and repair houses of people including those of the Yadavas. Only three families of this caste are craftsman, weaving clothes in their looms. The Yadavas and Brahmins do not purchase these clothes except a few napkins but most of the people of poor castes only go in for these clothes. The Yadavas engage the Julahas as agricultural labourers at the time of sowing and harvesting and for repairing their dwellings. At times the Julahas work in the field to weed out the grass and water the crops on daily wages.

Yadava, Laheri and Sonar

The Laheri preparers bangles and the Sonar ornamenets for the women folk in the village. Though the village Sonar does not make any beautiful and artistic ornaments, yet people remain contented with his work because he has his traditional monopoly in this profession. No doubt, the Yadavas and Brahmins as well as a few rich persons of other castes purchase ornaments from Bhagalpur but they do utilize his services for their washing and repairing.

Yadava, Halwai and Teli

The services of a Halwai are requisitioned on ceremonial occasions, particularly marriage and death, when feasts for a large number of people are organized. A Halwai prepares the Pakka food on such occasions for which he is paid in cash plus the food which he takes.

The Teli supplies mustard oil used in vegetables as well as to smear the body of a newly born body.

Yadava, Surhi and Baniya

The Baniyas and Surhis trade in grains. The Surhis mainly sell groceries but they do keep cosmatics, papers, pencils and medicines like Anacin, Aspro etc. in their shops. Though the Yadavas are self-sufficient in food yet they come to these shops for the purchase of many articles of daily use. Surhi women are famous for making Chura (Pressed rice) which has a good sale in the weekly market.

These things go to prove that each caste, directly or indirectly, works for the help of and support to others and, thereby, helps to maintain the structural unity and solidarity of the village. The reciprocity of relationship between one caste and the other is of unique importance for the study of social structure of a village community. However, to characterise the social relations existing between the different castes of the village as mutual and co-operative is only one part of the story. The other part of the story finds its manifestation in groups and factions, quarrel and conflict which jeopardize the integration of various castes into a stable social system. The instance of the Yadava and Brahmin can be cited. Outwardly, both are friendly to each other but, inwardly, both are in constant conflict.

Caste Mobility

Caste in the village records some significant modifications in different directions particularly in occupation, social distance, status, untouchability etc. Sanskritization and Westernization are slowly but steadily accelerating the process of change in the nature and functions of caste. The efforts of the lower caste to acquire the status of the higher caste and those of the untouchable caste to occupy the position of the lower caste are the recent trends towards caste mobility or fluidity. Caste consciousness and tension are the other highlights of caste dynamics discernible in the village. Today, caste retains only its endogamous character and, in other respects, undergoes the vast process of change.

Professor Srinivas (1966:7, 1955:17) clarifies the type of change which Sanskritization assuredly brings about in a particular caste. According to him-"Sanskritization is generally accompanied by, and often results in, upward mobility for the caste in question, but mobility may also occur without Sanskritization and vice versa. However, the mobility associated with Sanskritization results only in positional changes in the system and does not lead to any structural change."[10] Professor Dube observes the caste system as presenting 'only slight variations in some direction.' He (1955:224) views—"The caste system is still characterised by its traditional hierarchy, but some ineffective verbal protest can now be heard against it. Among the castes on the lower level of the agriculturist group there has been some effort made at rising in the social scale by the adoption of surnames and caste appellations traditionally belonging to the higher groups."[11] Finally, Professor Majumdar (1958:76) writes—"Towards speeding up the social capillarity and raising their caste status and position, another general tendency among the lower castes has been to adopt the ways of the higher castes."[12] Neither social relations in the village are characterised by the principle of superordination and subordination nor is position in the caste hierarchy determined by traditional occupation. Even Dhanuks and Surhis are Sanskritizing themselves by adopting the manners and customs of the higher castes.

Most of the lower castes have taken to agriculture after abandoning their traditional occupations with a view to raising their inferior caste status. Surprisingly enough, the Brahmins have also been found to have left their caste occupation and switched over to agriculture. At times it becomes difficult to find servicing caste in the village. In the past, Brahmins were given land by the Choudharies to settle in the village and in return, the former used to serve them on religious and ritual occasions. But today out of 39 Brahmin families only 10 families depend on Jajmani profession and the rest have taken to agriculture.

The modern means of transporation and communincation, improvement in agriculture, science, technology, industrialisation, urbanization etc. have played their decisive role in narrowing down the level of social distance between the different castes in the village. Besides, growth in trade, business and education has also promoted fluidity in caste. The lower and the untouchable castes do not tolerate the anger of the upper castes and try to raise their economic status with a view to coming up with them everywhere in the countryside.

Migration to towns and cities has resulted in the positional changes in the caste system of the village. A rich man or an officer of a lower caste is given a higher status compared to a common man belonging to a higher caste. The Surhis are of unclean caste, but because they are rich, they occupy the third position in the caste hierarchy of the village. No sooner a Yadava earns some money or acquires some land then he calls himself a Choudhary which indicates a shift in his status within the caste.

Adoption of Sanskritized titles and even of titles of the upper castes by the lower castes is a noticeable feature found in the village. The Kamars call themselves as Vishwakarma Pandit, Nais as Thakur Pandit, Dhanuks as Singh or Kshatriya, Julahas as Tantu Vaishya, Beldars as Bind, Dhobis as Rajak, Chamars as Rabidas, Dusadh as Dushashan Kshatriya, Surhis as Saundik Vaishya etc. The Yadavas, Baniyas, Surhis, Nais, Kumhars, Dhanuks and Beldars put on sacred thread and, to some extent, have adopted Brahmanic ways of life. The Jajmani relationship existing between the different castes in the village has changed into patron and client, master and tenant relationship. Bailey describes castes and caste-associations in the following manner : "The castes stand in a ritual and secular hierarchy, expressed in rules of interaction. One may take certain forms of cooked food only from members of the same caste or of a higher caste. To accept food, and in certain cases water, from a man of lower caste, is to be polluted."[13]

REFERENCES

CHAPTER III

1. Hutton, J.H., 1963, *Caste in India*, (Oxford University Press, Oxford House, Apollo Bunder, Bombay).

2. Panikkar, K.M., 1961,*Hindu Society at Cross Roads*, (Asia Publishing House, Bombay).

3. Risley, S.H., 1908, *The People of India*, (Thakers, Spink & Co., Calcutta).

4. *Ibid*,

5. Cox, O.C., 1959, *Caste, Class Aand Race*, (Monthly Review Press New York).

6. *Ibid.*

7. Majumdar, D.N., 1958, *Caste and Communication in an Indian Village*, (Asia Publishing House, Bombay).

8. Srinivas, M.N., 1955, '*The Social System of a Mysore Village*' *Village India*, (The University of Chicago Press, Chicago).

9. Mathur, K.S., 1964, *Caste and Ritual in Malwa Village*. (Asia Publishing House, Bombay).

10. Srinivas, M.N., 1966, *Social Change in Modern India*, (Allied Publisher, Bombay).

1955 *Ibid.*

11. Dube, S.C., 1955, *Indian Village*, (Routiedge & Kegan Paul Ltd, London).

12. *Ibid.*

13. Bailey, F.G., 1963, *Politics and Social Change : Orissa in 1959*, (University of California Press).

CHAPTER IV

Group Formation & Leadership Pattern

Importance of the Study

The study of group formation uncovers not merely the presence of small cohesive groups (called by Lewis as factions) — which remain as centres of authority and power, but also the very functioning of the village social organization. The study of these small groups constitutes a significant aspect of group dynamics in so far as it helps to analyse the behaviour pattern and value orientation of the members. Moreover, it is only through such a study that a close portrayal of village life (structural and functional change), tension and conflict, locus of authority and patterns of leadership is made possible. Emphasizing the useful significance of the study, Professor Majumdar (1958:86) observes: "A study of enduring and inclusive social groups has its importance not only in understanding and predicting the behaviour of its units, but also because such a structural analysis, combined with a functional study, gives some idea of the nature of the member's goals and the range of their behaviour possibilites...The manner in which the group behaviour occurs, or the study of group dynamics, throws much light on the form and the process of the community of which the group forms a part."[1] Professor Lewis (1958:113) thus puts forward his own views on the subject: "In our study of Rampur we discovered still another dimension of the social structure, and one which has received insufficient attention in the past; the existence of small cohesive groups within castes which are the locus of power and decision making and contribute to the compartmetalized and segmented nature of village organization. The study of these small groups takes us to the very heart of village life. It provides us with a key to the communications channels of the society and also reflects many of the values of the people."[2]

At the outset it is desirable to point out that the term 'faction' used by Professor Lewis for these social groups is not quite appropriate. In fact, they are basically lineage groups and are not formed simply for achieving political ends. The influence of political factor in the formation of these groups can not be denied, but that which is much more significant is the feeling of mutual understanding and cooperative undertaking. For the villagers, they are purely lineage groups (Khandan) which were in the past disunited or split from their original family due to quarrel and conflict. The size of these groups increases gradually with the rise in their population and the admission of defectors from other families and, in due course, they assume a large size which leads to further cleavages. Despite several forces and circumstances leading to ascendency, kinship remains the basis in the formation of groups.

In intergroup relations and communications, these groups are fundamentally held together by mutual understanding and cooperation. However, the bond of unity and fellow-feeling, which binds members of a single group, is conspicuously absent in other groups except on ceremonial occasions like marriage, funeral, general welfare of the community and its protection against outside attack. It is true that in the event of an inter-caste conflict, members of different groups within a caste tend to unite despite differences and meet the challenge unitedly. Earlier, it has been said that dissension and discord necessitate split in a group leading to the formation of new groups and alliances, but in case of any danger to the caste as a whole all of them will unite. It is much more cooperation and not conflict or hostility which regulates inter-group relations among members of different groups within a single caste.

The hypothetical formulation permeating the present discussion is that the size of kinship and the dominance of a group or its leadership are closely related. In other words, the bigger the size of kinship, the greater is its dominance and influence of leadership and conversely, the smaller the size, the lesser is its importance. Further, it has to be recalled that the Yadavas are the dominant caste at Bharko and in fact, the present research is based on this conceptual framework. Hence, discussion of group formation appears to be necessary from the standpoint of (1) testing the reliability of the hypothesis and (2) proving the dominance of the Yadava caste in the village. The following table indicates the distribution of Kinship groups among various castes at Bharko :—

TABLE No. 1

DISTRIBUTION OF GROUPS BY CASTE.

Caste	*Total Number of Families*	*Number of Groups*
Yadava	105	5
Brahmin	39	2
Surhi	50	3
Nai	12	1
Dhanuk	29	2
Julaha	22	1
Beldar	23	1
Chamar	63	3
Kumhar	11	1
	Total	19

A total of nineteen groups are shown in the above table; and of these the powerful and dominant are the five groups of the Yadavas. The behaviour possibilities of each of the five groups will be discussed on the subsequent pages. It has to be emphasized that the aforesaid groups are purely kinship groups and are not in a perpetual hostility towards each other. Some immigrant families of certain castes that are unable to form independent groups of their own for some reason or the other often align according to their convenience, with the existing caste groups. Such alignments within castes are primarily effected by neighbourhood and friendly relations. It is significant to note that the Kamars, Lohars, Baniyas, Sonars, Dusadhs, etc. have been unable to form independent blocks for the simple reason that they are not united by kinship ties. These castes get the support of their kin living outside the village on ceremonial and other important occasions. Hence, it is not so much the factor of economic backwardness or relationships with other castes (Jajmani relationships) or their being subservient to the upper castes as the absence of kinship relationship which is chiefly responsible for the absence of small cohesive groups within these castes in the village. However, Professor Lewis enumerates three conditions, namely cohesiveness, extensiveness and economic independence for the successful operation of caste factions.

Principal Groups Among the Yadavas

Numerically, the Yadavas are the strongest in the village with a total of 556 members in 105 families. The titlewise break up (for the sake of convenience) of 105 families is thus — Choudhary — 39, Mahto — 44, Mandal — 6, Yadava—3, Rai—3, Manjhi – 6 and Gope – 4. Except the Choudharies who are the original inhabitants of the village and of the neighbouring areas, the rest of the Yadavas are the immigrants in the village. Among the immigrants, some are related to the Choudharies through their daughter's marriage, some are to their son-in-laws, while the rest are the new comers. The following table illustrates the distribution of families by groups among the Yadavas :—

TABLE No. 2

DISTRIBUTION OF FAMILIES BY GROUPS AMONG THE YADAVAS

Group	*Number of families.*	*Number of aligned families.*	*Total number of families.*	*Total number of adult males*
B	16	30	46	65
A	11	...	11	37
C	18	...	18	32
D	16	...	16	25
E	10	4	14	18
Total :	71	34	105	177

In the above table B emerges as the strongest for being comprised of a total of 46 families with 65 adult males. In fact, it remains largely the central authority and decision-making body for the caste as a whole. Even in the organization of the village it exercises its political dominance.

C, when compared to D and E, proves to be influential and powerful not so much due to its large size but mainly due to its improved economic status. Except the supporting families in E, these three are also having close kinship ties among themselves.

TABLE No. 3

LAN OWNERSHIP AMONG THE PRINCIPAL GROUPS OF THE YADAVAS

Group	*Total number of families (both member & supporting)*	*Ownership of land in Bighas*	*Average per family.*
B	46	1175	25.5
A	11	500	45.4
C	18	300	16.6
D	16	80	5
E	14	25	1.7
Total :	105	2080	

In the above table the quantity of land owned by B excels that which is jointly held by all the four groups. The fact is is that a few families of ex-landlords and big cultivators belong to this group. In the village in respect of land, outside income, levels of living, social prestige and political dominance, B is supposed to be enjoying a much higher status than all other groups including A. The richest man, who was in the past the chief spokesman of the village and whose family, still exercises economic and political dominance within and outside his caste belongs to this group. Presently the younger son of this man, as his eldest son did in the past, holds the office of the Mukhiya (Headman) of the village.

Role of Kinship

Although in a rural area there are a number of contributing factors which account for the formation and sustenance of groups within castes, yet of these the most important is the factor of kinship. Quite a sufficient number of facts and studies support this contention. Closeness of kinship ties, at least among some of the families, is almost a prerequisite for the formation and sustenance of groups composed of more than one lineage. This is also applicable to those caste groups which are formed on the basis of factors other than kinship. In such circumstances when the group is possessed of more than one lineage, kinship and group may not be identical. The following table illustrates the distribution of lineage in the five groups of the Yadavas :

Table No. 4

DISTRIBUTION OF LINEAGE AMONG DIFFERENT YADAVA GROUPS.

Group	*Number of Families (Both Member and Aligned)*	*Number of Lineage*	*Number of Clans*
A	11	1	1
B	46	5	4
C	18	5	3
D	16	6	4
E	14	5	2
TOTAL :—	105	22	14

For an interpretation of the above table, a separate note, in an abridged form, on each of the groups is as under :

A, which consists of eleven families, is marked by close kinship ties because all its members are descendents of a common great-grand father. Both A and B, except the supporting families which joined B much later, come from the same lineage and clan and, as has been said earlier, since long these two have been functioning in the village as the most cohesive and enduring groups of the Yadavas.

B, which is composed of five lineages, has a total of forty-six families. Of this total, twenty-eight families—sixteen members and twelve supporting — are joined by close kinship bonds.

These families, though forming a separate group, bear close identity with A. The twelve supporting families in B were at one time with A, but they subsequently defected from it due to certain differences. The rest of the eighteen supporting families belong to four separate lineages and clans. Two groups, each consisting of six families, have their separate lineage and clan, whereas the other three groups, each consisting of three families, belong to the remaining two lineages. Despite kinship ties binding these groups separately, the families are unable to form their independent groups because they lack all those conditions required for the formation of groups. Hence, they have joined B which caters to their needs and interests.

C, which consists of eighteen member families, is composed of five lineages and two clans. Out of five, each one of the two lineages contains six families. Again, two more lineages have one family each but the remaining one has four families. Each group of six families in the first two lineages maintains friendly ties with some families in A and B. Families in the three lineages belonging to one clan are closely related whereas families in the remaining two lineages belonging to both the clans maintain friendly relationships. C, when compared to D and E, seems to have occupied a superior position in the socio-economic sphere and, therefore, functions as an independent group. The friendly ties existing between a few families in C and in A and B are reinforced by regular mutual economic transaction as well as close residence.

D, which comprises sixteen families, belongs to six lineages. Families in three of the lineages are from one clan whereas families in the remaining three lineages comprise of three different clans. Hence, relationship ties in the former are close and intimate, whereas in the latter they are not so. This group is considered as quite weak in maintaining its economic self-sufficiency or solidarity. As the families are exceedingly militant and contentious, the group occupies a lower status within the caste.

E is composed of ten members and four supporting families which belong to five lineages and two clans. Four of the lineages are maintaining close ties, whereas the remaining one is having only friendly relationship. All the families are clustered together at one place. It is much more the factor of close residences or cultural participation on ceremonial occasions, than inter-relationship between lineages, which is important in the formation of this group. The last two groups are not as much cohesive and enduring as the first two are. These points finally lead to the discovery of the following factors found to be instrumental in the formation of groups at Bharko :—

1. Kinship;
2. Residence at one place ;
3. Frindly relations ;
4. Common interest ;
5. Fear of insecurity ; and
6. Participation in common cultural activities.

Inter-Group Relations

It is really very difficult to present a detailed study of the varied relationship existing among the groups or factions within caste because the informants, as it were, felt fearful of divulging something as inner to an outsider. It was with much difficulty that some facts could be gathered on the subject. In the brief history presented earlier in the Second Chapter references have been made to the facts and circumstances leading to the acquisition of landlordism by the Choudharies of the village. Choudharies, who descended from one single but old geneological stock, were the first inhabitants of the region surrounding the village. It was they who, in the beginning, invited a few Jajmani castes and offered them land to settle in the village. In the process of time, the number of castes increased and the village assumed a multi-caste character. In the past the caste had no group or faction, rather the whole of it constituted one solid and powerful group. It was only some hundred years ago that the families were split, for the sake of social conveniences, into two groups, A and B. The inter-group relations existing between these two groups were chiefly characterised by mutual understanding and cooperation and it was rarely that any tension or conflict occurred between them.

The circumstances prevailing today are quite different from what they were in the past. Not simply cooperation but conflict as well influences their inter-group relations. In fact, on many occasions, both the groups have been engaged in a trial of strength resulting in several injuries and bloodsheds. Several instances of litigation, filed in the local courts, between a few families belonging to both the groups, can be cited in support of the above notion. Both are inimical to each other as they constantly struggle for their dominance and power. B, on account of its large size and the solid economic position of its constituent families, has emerged as more powerful than A. Nevertheless, the importance of A, which is thought to be equally powerful, is also recognized by all the groups within the caste. In the overall organization of the village both A and B jointly prevail upon all other castes in the village.

As time and circumstances immensely influence intergroup relations, it is very difficult to evolve lasting sets of relationships between the various groups in the village. For instance, if a group has maintained friendly relationship with another group for a particular period of time, the same group may have, at a subsequent period, hostility towards the other, if the situations so warrant. Hence, the degree of relationship varies in different periods of time and in different situations. Shift of members from one group to another and end of hostility between the groups in certain situations are a few glaring cases which support the notion. The groups under study are characterised by three sets of relationships, namely, friendship, hostility and neutrality. As A and B are collaterals, their interrelations are outwardly characterised by friendship and cordiality, and inwardly by srong feeling of hostility. For fear of social criticism by their caste leaders and others outside the caste, both pose to be friendly in their daily meeting or conversations and exchange of visits during illness or other catastrophes but, inwardly both strive for each other's ruin or annihilation.

A is jealous of B's prosperity and wealth, and confrontation between them is mainly due to the latter's oppressive attitude and deceitful nature. However, the main conflict of the Choudhary is with the Brahmin known as Thakur in the village. It is true that in the wake of any conflict arising between a Choudhary and a Thakur, all the groups (in that sense the whole caste) will unite to face the opposite party. In the village, there are mainly three parties, namely, Yadava, Brahmin and Surhi and of these the strongest is the Yadava.

Recently, C is on friendly terms with both A and B. One group of six families in C has intimacy with the same number of families in A and again, another group of eight families in C fosters friendly relationship with the equal number of families in B. The concerned families invite reciprocally only the male members to the ceremonial feasts in marriage and death. But the friendship that exists between these families is not very intimate, and the same is based on a political consideration rather on a social or cultural participation.

D and E are in many respects similar though both constitute distinct groups. Members of these groups are economically and culturally backward; and are serviceable to the Choudharies or to the Brahmins in agricultural operation as their tenants and labourers. Because of their weak economic position, they do not usually interfere in other's affairs nor do they have any courage to do so. Consequently, both the groups function as neutral groups within the caste. However, they inwardly hate A and B for their oppressive and tyrannical nature.

Notwithstanding the improved economic and social position of the Yadavas, they are widely known in this part of the country for their cultaral backwardness. Contrarily, the Choudharies of the village and of the surrounding areas are reputed for their economic and cultural advancement. If not all, at least a few families in A and B are exceedingly well mannered and are, therefore, respected or liked by all the castes including the Brahmin in the village and outside.

Process of Group Formation

For a good grasp of the process of group formation it is necessary that the major conflicting events should be presented. In the preceding pages, a passing reference to some such events has been made; however, something more on the subject has yet to be discussed. Nearly hundred years ago a dispute regarding ownership of Ghatwali land occurred among the Choudharies, which ultimately led to the division of the group into A and B. Once it happened that one member in A give land measuring 1284 bighas to a member in B and made him his tenant. Gradually the latter started establishing his ownership over that land and stopped paying land rent to the former who ultimately took away the land from the latter's possession. Later on, the tenant with his five brothers and a few of his men armed with lathis (bamboo sticks) and bhalas (spares) went to the site of the plot to occupy it. Confrontation between the parties took place in which a few of his men received serious injuries and thus they were all driven away. The tenant filed a case in the local court for the restoration of his ownership of that land but (there also) he lost it. Since then both A and B are functioning as two independent groups, inwardly engineering jealousy and hatred towards each other.

Again, once four persons, two from each of the above groups, were playing cards at somebody's house. A few spectators, including one brother-in-law of a member in group A, were also present. In course of the play, the said brother-in-law unnecessarily exhibited a pride of his wealth and by the way criticised another man, supposed to be the wealthiest of all in B. That infuriated the two members pressent who, replying on behalf of the wealthiest man, said that even on the skirts of his sister's house he would find himself standing on the land of the man he had criticised. A serious confrontation between the two groups occurred on the issue in which some persons were injured.

The jealousy between the two groups mounted and each of them made efforts to take revenge upon the other. It was B which first got an opportunity to avenge its insult on A. One Julaha wanted to put up an enclosure around his house on the roadside. This was objected to by that very man who fought with the leader of group B on the plea that the enclosure would make the road to his house all the more narrow and also make the movements of his carts impossible. The leader of group B helped the Julaha in fencing his house and instructed him to beat back if any member from grom group A should put any further objection. A clash took place between the Julaha and members of A in which members of B fought on behalf of that Julaha and ultimately helped him in erecting the enclosure.

Again, a widow, belonging to a Brahmin caste, sold hér house and land to an influential member of group A. The leader of group B felt jealous of it because he wanted the property of that woman to be sold to him. Out of disappointment, he promised the Brahmins that the would help them if they did not allow the purchaser to take possession of the house and land. The purchaser with his men went to take possession of the house but they were all severely beaten up by the Brahmins backed by members of group B. Ultimately, the fellow took shelter of the Court which passed a decree in his favour but influential persons in group B requested him to leave the property with the woman as she was a poor widow to which he readily agreed. The fellow neither got the property nor his money.

C, D and E were formed quite lately. As has been stated earlier, they consist of the families of Bhaginmans, who, in the beginning, came from different places to settle in the village. In the past, all the families in C were aligned with A and B but, when subjected to humiliation and criticism, they defected from these groups and formed an independent group for themselves. Similarly, families in D and E, which were at one time aligned with C, formed their own independent groups. The families in C are self-made or are otherwise economically well off. Perhaps, this very factor of economic independence has emboldened them to form a separate group with a view to getting freedom from humiliation and unnecessary harassment. Though, in the beginning, a clash of interests must have been instrumental in its defection from A and B, yet, unlike the other two groups, it now receives an equal treatment both from A and B since it has improved its economic strength within the caste.

D came into being as a result of conflict with two families in C. The quarrel started over the stoppage of canal-water for irrigational purposes. During the rainy season, villagers raise Chitka (upright pieces of small wood) at the mouth of a stream or canal to irrigate their land. There is a time-limit to such an erection prescribed for the cultivators. Two persons in C were irrigating their land through that process beyond the time allotted to them. One person in D, who was also in need of canal-water for his land, requested them to open the Chitka but they did not listen to him. When they went away he opened the Chitka with the result that a serious conflict occurred in which one man received fatal injuries. The incidence, which happened about ten years ago, led to the formation of D because the families in it thereafter did not feel it worthwhile to remain with the families in C.

E was formed purely on the basis of common residences. A few families in E, which were previously aligned with D, defected from it on some minor conflicting issues or due to certain differences. Afterwards, for the sake of convenience they formed their own independent group of families living in close proximity to each other or in the same neighbourhood. Hence, common residences to great measure necessitated the formation of E as a separate group. Besides, defection is caused due to dissension and discord which emanate from :

(a) encroachment on land,

(b) stoppage of canal-water from flowing into other's land for Patawan (irrigational purposes),

(c) unauthorized sale or purchase of land,

(d) dispute over any debacle in the queue of men making goat-sacrifice in the Bhagawati Asthan on the Dashera day, and finally,

(e) village politics.

Quarrels generally arise out of personal, ritual and economic factors which ultimately involve the groups or the castes. In his study of Shivapur, K. Ishwaran (1966:96) observes — "When the individual transgresses the rules of marriage, kinship, occupation and ritual, his life is plunged into conflict with the social moves, thus leading to acute tensions".[3] According to him the following sources give rise to personal quarrels :—

(1) land

(2) impact of competition from outside,

(3) failure of crops due to shortage of rainfall,

(4) population pressure,

(5) property, and

(6) ideological factors.

In my study of Bharko I have also discovered equally the same sources as giving rise to tension and conflict between one individual and the other. At times serious conflicts lead to boycott of invitation on ceremonial occasions and discontinuance of mutual conversation between the families concerned. In the village, these processes are, no doubt, instrumental in the formation of new factions or groups within caste.

Leadership Pattern

Leadership is based on several factors such as age, wealth, family background, kindness, honesty, education, outside contact, etc; but the basic factor involved is the size of family and lineage. The value of this factor is preeminently recognized when there is the dominance of a single group or groups within caste. It is mainly on account of this factor that B and A have been successful in excercising their social and political dominance over all other castes in the village. Although the Brahmins at Bharko have emerged as the second equally dominant caste, which infrequently gives the impression that the village perhaps has two dominant castes, each diametrically opposed to the other, yet, the village social organization in its internal aspect establishes the fact of the Yadavas being dominant. Even among small groups within caste which consist of either families of close kin of one lineage or those of relatives and friends of different lineages, leaders are generally chosen from amongst members having support of a large family belonging to one lineage. Finally, it has been found that in a rural community a person who gets the support of a minimum of ten families forms a group and becomes its leader. By far this applies to the selection of leaders of small groups within castes but this guides the people even in their selection of village leaders in whom they become anxious to discover first no other trait except the support of certain number of families.

The striking feature of leaders is their compatible higher socio-economic status. As leadership and wealth go side by side, it is not uncommon if this privilege is enjoyed by the rich persons in the community. An increase in wealth accompanies mobility of social and economic nature in the status of a person or his family. A wealthy person draws several members around him, who are prepared to render him service in all exigencies such as standing as witness in Court cases, extending physical help in any type of dispute, making arrangements on ceremonial occasions, etc. In return, these people receive help and protection from him. They seek his practical and useful advice even on trifle matters. Thus, the situations in which a rich man becomes a leader in rural community are self-evident. In the village, such persons are regarded as prominent figures and it is they who form the centre of authority and power for the eommunity as a whole. At Bharko this pattern of leadership is provided by the two castes — Yadava and Brahmin.

The table below indicates the distribution of group leaders by age and caste.

TABLE NO 5

DISTRIBUTION OF GROUP LEADERS BY AGE AND CASTE

CASTE

Age group	Vadava	Brahmin	Surhi	Beldar	Chamar	Dhobi	Kumhar	Dhanuk	Nai	Kamar	Julaha	Total
1	2	3	4	5	6	7	8	9	10	11	12	13
25-35	1	x	1	1	1	x	x	x	x	x	x	4
36-46	4	2	2	1	1	1	1	2	1	1	1	17
47-57	x	2	x	x	x	x	x	1	x	x	x	3
Total :	5	4	3	2	2	1	1	3	1	1	1	24

For a person striving for the achievement of the status of a leader, age is an important factor. Though in the past, one's age was considered as an essential qualification for leadership, yet to-day the same does not receive much attention. This, however, does not mean that villagers have no respect for age. The table presented above supports the view that the villagers still have respect for age; nevertheless, the recent trend is towards preference for young leaders, supposed to be well-informed and much more capable than the old ones. It is interesting to note that the present Mukhiya (Headman) of the official village Panchayat is a young man of only twenty-eight years of age. Out of a total of 24 leaders, 4 belong to the age group of 25-35, 17 to the age of 36-46 and only 3 to the age group of 47-57.

Another important qualification which the vlllagers desire to find out in their leaders is their family background. It is obvious that a person who comes of a respectable family has a fairer chance for leadership than those who fail to fulfil this requirement. The reputation of one's family depends on several factors, but those that are important are — improved socio-economic status, education, caste, humility, hospitality and respect for persons around it. However, in the eyes of people reputation of one's family also depends upon the types of relations and friends and their status as well as the amount of money spent during marriage of sons and daughters. As the families of the Choudharies and also of the Brahmins are well-reputed, this very fact keeps their leadership in a secured position.

Recently, spread in education has brought about a significant change in the structure of leadership. Knowledge of reading and writing is considered as the essential qualification for a leader. It is good if the leader is educated. The present Mukhiya has read upto B.A. standard of the Bhagalpur University whereas his predecessor, a pretty old man, had no schooling at all. For this reason old and illiterate leaders are not preferred these days.

Outside influence and contact with influential persons precipitate one to the position of a leader. Of the five leaders among the Yadavas, one is associated with the Congress Party and is closely known to ministers and officials in the State Government. Besides, one's personal relationship with the people around him is also important in bringing him to the forefront. Villagers do not like persons of tyrannical nature as well as those who are dishonest or deceitful for the position of a leader. But one who is impartial, just, kind and honest is readily preferred for the position of authority and power. In a nutshell, patterns of leadership depend upon many factors as mentioned above.

At Bharko there are mainly two categories of leaders —

(1) Caste leaders, and

(2) Panchayat leaders.

Both these two types of leaders are characterised by Lewis (1958 : 128) as 'Primary' and 'Secondary'. Both serve different functions. The former performs the political function whereas the latter fulfils the social obligation. In this connection it has to be stressed that there has not been much change in the structure of leadership pattern. In the case-study of Kannari Mura, a village in Japan, S. Seshaiah's findings (1966 : 19) are worth mentioning. He observes — 'that the basic structure of leadership has not undergone much change. The pre-reform leaders still have control in many spheres of local affairs. But the change or stability in the structure becomee meaningful, only when seen in relation to its process." This is also true to the structure of leadership in the Indian countryside.

Caste Panchayats

Caste Panchayats now no longer play any vital role in the social organization of a village. In most of the villages they are not even heard of and if at all they exist, they perform meaningless functions. Forces which have raged this organization are countless, but those that are basically responsible for their wreckage are the modern social and political forces. In the past, caste panchayats used to perform several functions—ranging from imposition of fine and ex-communication to the execution of proposals for ameliorating the general conditions of their castes. Today also, wherever they exist they perform these functions but no attention is obviously paid to them. Removal of untouchability, gain of economic independence, social awakening, outside contact with towns and cities, besides urbanisation and industrilization, promote non-conformity to caste rules and prescriptions. Perhaps for these reasons caste panchayats have become defunct. However, the following castes at Bharko still possess caste Panchayats —

> Yadava, Surhi, Chamar, Julaha, Beldar, Nai, Gorhi, Dhanuk, Kumhar and Dhobi

but they do not justify their existence because they preeminently perform political functions than the social functions.

Througout the country, villages to-day are factionridden. Mounting inter-caste rivalry has made life in the countryside tiresome and burdensome. In such situations caste leadeas are required to discharge responsible obligations towards their castemen. They discuss policy matters pertaining to their castes and strive for resolving internal differences which threaten their unity and solidarity. If one caste oppresses the other, strategy which the latter has to adopt is often decided by its leaders. In case of direct conflict between two castes, members of both the castes face each other unitedly. In addition, the caste leaders bring about reforms aiming at removing the evils of their caste.

Village Panchayats

In pursuance of the Bihar Panchayat Raj Act of 1957, a four-village Panchayat was established at Bharko on the 2nd October, 1954. In the first and second elections of the Mukhiya and the Surpanch (incharge of judiciary) which took place on the 14th April, 1960 and on the 26th December, 1963 respectively, a total of 2004 and 2239 voters exercised their franchise. After the elections of the Mukhiya and the Surpanch, the Up-Mukhiya and the Up-Surpanch were subsequently elected. Each of the two bodies — the executive and the judiciary, consisted of 9 members including the headman and the surpanch respectively. The highlight of the aforesaid elections was that both executive heads were from amongst the Yadavas and were elected unanimously. Besides, under the Panchayat, one viliage formed one constituency or ward and one representative from each of the four constituencies was elected to both the wings of the Panchayat. The remaining four members were nominated by the Mukhiya and the Surpanch for their respective cabinets. According to the Act, one seat was reserved for a female member, though the Panchayat did not have any female member in either of the two wings. In the recent elections, the Office of the Mukhiya has gone to a Yadava and that of the Surpanch to a Surhi.

As the Panchayat Bhawan (building) is still under construction, the Office of the Panchayat is located in a two-roomed pucca house known to the people as their Zamindar's Kutchery (Court) where the latter's Patwari (accountant) used to collect Malgujari (land revnue) from them. The Office of the

Panchayat is actually kept in a small room of that house as its other room is occupied by a Government Karmachari (Accountant) who is incharge of village land records. The Panchayat holds its regular meetings usually on the Verandah of the house.

The Village Panchayat aims at fulfilling several important functions and obligations. Its aims and objectives have been outlined in the first and the second five year plans. Emphasizing the need of training of villagers in village administration, the Second Five Year Plan (1956:151) outlines the following reasons for its significance :—

> "The development of village Panchayats on the right lines has significance for several reasons, under the impact of new developments, including the growth of population, land reform, urbanization, spread of education, increase in population and improvement in communications, village society is in a state of rapid transition. In emphasizing the interest of the community as a whole and in particular the needs of those sections which are at present handicapped in various ways, village panchayats along with cooperatives, can play a considerable part in bringing about a more just and integrated social structure in rural areas and in developing a new pattern of rural leadership."[6]...

The important question — as to how far has the above objective as envisaged in the Plan been achieved in the village, deserves careful examination. Empirical studies, on the contrary, reveal something as startling and gloomy about the workings of these panchayats. Retzlaff (1962:4) in a case study of the village government in Khalapur comes to this finding —

> "Marked disparity in economic and social status had traditionally concentrated political power in the hands of a relatively small rural elite. The manner in which these new Institutions were brought into being did little, at the outset, to alter the power position of that rural elite. This virtually negated the possibility of the panchayats becoming the agents of radical social and economic change,

or of serving as the vehicles for the rapid introduction of democratic principles and procedures into rural life...where less privileged social groups begin to openly support change, it was exceedingly difficult for them to wrest control of these new institutions from the tradi-oriented elite."[7]

However, Retzlaff feels optimistic about future improvements in the situation provided sufficient attention is paid by the government. He (1962:10) writes —

"Studies by sociologists and anthropologists (as well as the author's own personal observation) bear witness to the fact that the existence of what is loosely termed factionism within a dominant caste in a village has led necessity of one or the other faction seeking the support of lower caste elemennts in such things as village panchayat elections. As a price for this support some change, however modest, is made in the position of these lower caste groups, both in terms of tangible economic rewards, as well as in less tangible alterations in status relationships."[3]

But writing the preface to Malaviya's book on village panchayats, Mr. Sriman Narayan (1956:XIV) cautions the planner thus —

"There is, however, one point which requires rethinking It has been recently pointed out by Acharya Vinobaji and others that the village Panchayats in India would really succeed in bringing about decentralization of economic and political power only if we take early steps to create conditions for greater social and economic equality in our countryside. Village Panchayats in a society, which is still dominated by various types of vested interests, may become insturuments of oppression rather than agencies for quick social and economic reform."[9]

It is a fact that the situations described above are still inherent in the structure of authority and power in a majority of the Indian villages. The situations described by A.R. Beals

(1955:89) about Namhalli between 1900-1914 are not obtainable in the present-day village Society.

Today, authority and leadership of the village are vested not in any individual leader rather in the whole of the statutory village Panchayat, However, this does not negate the powerful influence of the various caste or faction leaders in the village. In actual practice these leaders are genuinely active and powerful than the Panchayat leaders. The panchayat leaders, who are often the caste or faction leaders, are vehemently opposed by the latter and commonly this fact leads to chaos in the Panchayat administration or failure of the village development programmes. At Bharko, as in other villages, the success of development works depends upon the joint approval of both the caste and Panchayat leaders. If a common agreement is not reached at, the progress of the viliage remains at standstill. Albert Mayer (1958:222:223) in his pilot study of rural development at Etawah discovers the same thing—

> "Factional leadership is often apparent and active in Indian villages. Village factions or 'parties' in U.P. are famous and feared, and often are so bitterly opposed to each other that an impasse is reached on issues of vital importance to the community as a whole. The existence of factions cannot be denied or ignored."

Further, K. Ranga Rao (1996:51:52) in his study of a village in Visakhapatnam in Andhra Pradesh illustrates as to how the existence of factional leadership obstructs and hampers the development work of the Panchayat. He describes, —

> "The present Panchayat was unanimously elected early in 1964. But it is very inactive. Its members were selected from among the so-called neutrals keeping the active leaders out of the Panchayat. As it is, the present Panchayat feels unable to undertake any development activity—even repairs of roads for want of support from the active leaders of the village who are split in two rival groups since early 1961."

This fact is largely applicable to Bharko which has mainly three strong parties besides a few small and weak ones. The existence of these caste factions obstructed the Panchayat in providing the village with the so-called 'structured' leadership.

Even cases of conflicts and disputes are mutually settled and decided by the primary or faction leaders before they are referred to the Panchayat. It is interesting to note that between 1960-65 there were in all 54 cases — 7 Civil and 47 criminal, reported to the Panchayat, yet most of them were from villages other than Bharko.

REFERENCES

CHAPTER IV

1. Majumdar, D.N., 1958, *Case and Communication in an Indian Village.*, (Asia Publishing House, Bombay).

2. Lewis, Oscar, 1958, *Village Life in Northern India.* (University of Illinois Press Urbana, U.S.A).

3. Ishwaran, 1966, *Tradition and Economy in Village India*, (Allied Publishers Pvt. Ltd. Bombay).

4. *Ibid.*

5. Seshaiah, S, 1966, *'Post-War Reforms and Changes in the Leadership Structure of Village Japan—A Case study*, Eastern Anthropologist, (The Ethnographic & Folk-Culture Society (U.P.), Lucknow (India)).

6. Second Five Year Plan, 1966, Government of India, (Planning Commission.

7. Retzlaff, R.H., 1962, *Village Government in India*, (Asia Publishing House, Bombay).

8. *Ibid.*

9. Malviya, H.D., 1956, *Village Panchayats in India*, Economic & Political Research Department, All India Congress Committee, New Delhi.

10. Beals, A.R. 1955 '*Interplay among Factors of Change in a Mysore Village*' Village India, Ed. by Mckim Marriott. (University of Chicago Press, Chicago, U.S.A).

11. Mayer, A, 1958, *Pilot Project, India*, (University of California Press, Chicago, U.S.A).

12. Ranga Rao, K., 1966, '*Leadership in a Community Development Village*'—Sociological Aspects of Community Development. Ed. by M.V. Moorthy, Deptt. of Sociology & Social Work; Andhra University, Waltair.

CHAPTER V

Economic Structure

Caste and Village Economy

The study of economic structure by a sociologist or an anthropologist, engaged in research into socio-cultural change in a village community, is considered as quite indispensable. The significance of this approach is exclusively felt for having a microscopic examination of the degree of relationship between the economic organization and the social system of a particular community. The interest of a sociologist or an anthropologist is, therefore, centred not in its land-tenure, revenue system, population pressure and method of production, rather in the patterns of economic behaviour in relation to its social organization. For an explanation of this issue, a brief discussion on the ties between caste and economic structure is presented below.

Despite several changes in the village, caste is still identified by its traditional occupation and specialized function. Quoting a passage from F.G. Bailey's Caste and the Economic Frontier, M.N. Srinivas (1966:90) thus supports this fact —

> "The handling of hides and skins is traditionally done by the Untouchable castes, and here is a good example of caste providing a monopoly."[1]

These monopolised occupations and functions of caste are closely linked with the community's economic structure. Even the Jajmani system, as prevalent in a village, has its moorings in economic considerations. Variations in caste status occur due to several factors but possession of land acquisition of wealth is locally considered as a basic factor. F.G. Bailey (1955:127) shows how the Boad Distillers of Phulbani in Orissa rose up from their previous position of a low caste to their present position of a high caste i.e. second to the Warriors. He observes, —

> "The Boad men have found recognition of a new economic status by rising within the caste and political systems of the village. They have neither rebelled and sought to place themselves at the head of the system nor have they staged a revolution and tried to overthrow the system They have acquired power commensurate with their wealth by using constitutional means, so to speak."[2]

Though the emergence of a purely economic class is still quite remote in the village, a gradual rise in the caste status caused by economic changes introduces a new phenomenon in caste dynamics in rural India. M.N. Srinivas (1966:117) refers to these changes in the following passage, —

> "The emergence of the big and powerful castes, the great occupational heterogeneity within each of them, the keen competition between castes for political and economic power, the spread of equalitarian ideology, and increasing political and social mobilization-all suggest that changes of a fundamental kind are occurring."[3]

To those who are interested in an intensive study of the problem, an economic inventory for the village will always be helpful, though the same is not required here. Earlier, in the Chapter on 'Caste Structure' much has been said about Jajmani relations among various castes in Bharko, nevertheless, a passing reference to the system needs its presentation here as well. Unquestionably, it is much more the economic transaction than the socio-cultural integration among various castes that constitutes the core of the Jajmani system. Among the Yadavas, mostly the Chowdharies are the big land owners and therefore, in the economic field, they excercise inordinate dominance over all other castes in the village. This prompts a constellation of occupational, landless and artisan castes doing a number of economic services to the Choudharies. In the economic hierarchy of the village, the Brahmins occupy the second position and the Surhis the third. Thus the Kamars make plough, bullock carts, wooden doors, chairs, cots etc. The Lohar repairs and supplies blades, khurpa, sickle and other agricultural tools and implements. The Chamars and the Jolahas invariably work as plough-men for the rich castes. The Beldrs and the Dusadhs serve them as agricultural labourers. In all weathers and with all dexterity peasants and labourers, specialized in various caste and economic occupations, render services to the landowning castes and are served by them. Thus, the integration of various castes in the economic organization leads to a kind of stable village unity or solidarity.

If agriculture contributes to the maintenance and support of caste in a rural area, the contribution of caste towards the success of agriculture is likewise invaluable. Tradition imposes certain economic and service obligations on each caste and it is through these services that agriculture is carried on in the village. It is not denying the fact that majority of the villagers, irrespective of wheather they possess land or not, depend on agriculture for their subsistence and livelihood. This builds mutual co-operation among various castes in agricultural activities. When the castes structure changes, mutual economic co-operation between the castes also undergoes a change. A.C. Mayer (1952:51) refers to such type of change in this manner, —

> "Caste is growing weaker in towns than in villages, and remains stronger among the uneducated and older people. As the caste structure crumbles, so relations among groups on the land, hitherto largely governed by caste, become less standardized, and different land interest are less equated with the different castes."[4]

The number of persons or families engaged in various caste and economic occupations in Bharko, with transfers or shifts from their traditional occupations, is proposed to be presented in the concluding pages of the Chapter.

Land

The net area of the village as shown in government records is 3526:74 acres. Out of this, the total area of cultivable land comes to 2387:57 acres and that of uncultivable land to 1139:17 acres. According to the available records, the distribution of uncultivable waste land is thus :

Permanent barren land	—	465:174,
Forest	—	88:71,
Orchard	—	6:92,
Graveyard	—	0:71,
Dhanaur (Nala)	—	20:14,
Bhir	—	5:26,
River	—	26:50,
Ditch	—	0:24,
Embankment	—	16:32,
Temple	—	0:67,
Road	—	20:73,

Pond — 7:68 acres, etc. The net area of wet or irrigated land comes to 1825.21 acres and that of the dry or unirrigated land comes to 562.36 acres. These figures clearly indicate that the area of irrigated land is much larger than that of unirrigated. In other words, it establishes that the sources of irrigation in the village are many. The following table indicates the area of irrigated land with types of crops :

TABLE No. 1

Land.	*Bhadai.*	*Agrahani.*	*Rabi,*	*Summer.*	*Total*
Irrigated	25.14	1729:81	66.11	4.15	1825.21
Unirrigated	274.99	25,37	257.87	4.13	562.36
Total :	300.13	1755.18	323.98	8.28	2387.57

The distinction between common and private land also exists in Bharko and the traditional function of common land as defined by Lewis (1958:93) is applicable to it.

Traditionally, the common land serves collective purposes such as, the grazing of cattle and the provision of wood. The village land is quite fertile for the all types of crops but mainly for paddy, wheat, maize and sugarcanc. There is a great demand for agricultural land in the village. The price of a good paddy land has increased within the last fifteen years from Rs. 1000 to Rs. 5000 per Bigha. There is no pasturing or grazing land in the village. The common land includes the inhabitant land, ponds, pools, school, road, ditch etc. which are generally revenue free.

The total area of private land on which revenue must be paid is 2387:57 acres. Thouth road ceass education tax are also included in the revenue, yet, for the whole Mauja, the agricultural tax alone comes to about Rs. 9000. The first settlement was made in the year 1905 when the revenue was proportionately quite nominal. Since then, several changes in land-use patterns have occured all over the country. Today the work of revenue collection is done by the State Government through the village Panchayat as the Zamindari system is no longer in existence.

Bharko may be desingnated as what Badden-Powell calls-'Joint Village'. The whole Mauja, including several of its hamlets, was accountable for the payment of revenue in lump sum. The Kutchery (as is still known) was originally the office of the Zamindar's Patwari who used to collect revenue for the whole mauja. The following statement shows the recent demand and collection of revenue from this mauja.

As has been said before, since the abolition of the Zamindari system, the village Panchayat, under the authority delegated to it, collects revenue for the State Government. Now, whether the abolition of Zaminadari has given relief to the farmers or not needs careful examination by the economists as the issue entails both satisfaction and dissatisfaction among the tenants.

STATEMENT OF ANNUAL DEMAND AND COLLECTION OF REVENUE AT BHARKO—(1961-66)

Year	*Arrear in Rs.*	*Current in Rs.*	*Total in Rs.*	*Rent Arrear*	*Collection Current*	*Road Cess Coll. Arr.*	*Road Cess Coll. Curr.*	*Edu. Cess Coll. Arr.*	*Edu. Cess Coll. Curr.*
1961-62.	3230.02	1554.85	4784.87	2778.19	1320.00	205.14	117.25	219.42	117.63
1962-63.	16344.19	4373.56	20717.75	14419.08	3852.91	1168.03	268.96	756.36	251.67
1963-64.	6204.7	2945.33	9149.40	5448.43	2526.22	408.51	210.12	346.62	208.99
1964-65.	1791.82	6729.70	8521.58	1583.43	6022.18	108.40,	300.50	99.99	317.08
1965-76.	5380.96	2539.98	7920.94	4782.38	2230.15	324.18	158.43	274.43	151.43

Land reform legislation like ceilings on land, transfer of land, mortgage, credit, proprietor and Bhoodan and Sarvoday, improved methods of agriculture etc. are important issues that need particular attention of economists.

Agriculture

Though the villagers count four seasons in the agricultural year, yet two of them, namely—Bhadai and Rabi, are considerably important. The remaining two are known as Agrahani and Garma (Summer crops). Bhadai is from the Hindu month Bhadra (August-September) and Agrahani from Agrahan (November-December). Bhadai crops, also known as Kharif crops, depend on heavy down-pour caused by the monsoon, whereas Rabi crops depend on light rains. However, in case of drought (as is the case in the present year) the prospect of these crops depends entirely on sources of irrigation.

Agricultural Year

For Bhadai crops, the sowing season begins from the month of Vaisakh (April-May) and is over by the end of Jyestha (May-June). It takes about three months for the crops to ripen when they are finally harvested in Bhadra (August-September). The crops raised during the period include paddy, maize, mahua, jute, pulse(Mung) etc. Sowing for the Agrahani crops begins in Bhadra (August-September), whereas harvesting starts from the month of Agrahan (November-December). The main crops raised during the period are paddy, arhar, kalai and maize. Rabi crops (also known as Chaita) are sown consecutively for three months — Kartik, Agrahan and Paush and are harvested in the month of Chaitra (March-April). The main crops of the season are wheat, barley, gram, millet, chikna, khesari, masur, oil seeds, etc. Garma crops mostly include tuber crops grown on sandy soil during summer season

Paddy, wheat and sugarcane are thought to be the main crops as they are grown in sufficiently large acreage of land. The work of paddy plantation begins in the rainy season. For a cultivator good rains mean good crops and better yields, whereas drought means famine or starvation. A favourable monsoon, therefore, is the chief expectation of the people in the countryside. Though a little rain is essential for all varieties of crops, yet for paddy heavy down-pour is needed. Paddy seeds are first broad-cast in a small piece of land; afterwards seedlings are planted when sufficient water remains accumulated in the field, after a bit of rainfall, sowing of maize and arhar also begins during this period.

Rabi crops are sown immediately after paddy and maize are harvested. After rice, the stable food consumed by the people is bread made of wheat. Wheat, barley, millet, pulse, peas, oil seeds, etc. require scanty rains and, if necessary, sources of irrigation are also utilised for this purpose. After two or three ploughings, seeds are scattered all over the field which take a bit of time to germinate in the soil. In addition to paddy and wheat, sugarcane is also a major crops and is raised on a pretty scale in this part of the State. There are 33 sugar mills at Amarpur, place of business for sugar and gur, besides rice and wheat. Such mills, where sugarcane is deposited for preparation of its juice, are commonly seen in the surrounding areas including the village under study. Tobacco is grown in the village for personal consumption only.

Crops

According to the estimates of the Gramsewak and the village level worker, the area of land in which major crops are grown is thus :

Paddy — 1740 Acres,

Wheat — 82 acres, and

Sugarcane (Cash Crop) — 32 acres.

The area in which minor crops are raised is as follows: —

Gram — 254 acres

Maize — 113 acres

Barley — 16 acres

Oilseeds — 12 acres, and

Potato — 40 acres.

Wheat is grown on almost the same land and in about the same acreage of land in which paddy is grown. Common crop rotation, like paddy followed by Chaita and maize followed by Rabi, is usually practised in the village and this is very important as 3/4th of the paddy land is utilised for such rotation. The following table indicates the estimated average yield of crops procured from a few progressive cultivators in the village :

Crops	*Yield per Bigha in Maunnds.*	*Price per Maund in Rs.*
1. Major Crops		
(a) Paddy	10	40
(b) Wheat	4	75
2. Minor Crops		
(a) Barley	3	60
(b) Gram	2	80
3. Pulses		
(a) Arhar	5	75
(b) Matar	2	65
(c) Khesari	2	60
(d) Tisi	3	85
(e) Masur	4	80
(f) Kalai	3	80
(g) Kurthi	4	60
4. Cash Crops		
(a) Sugarcane	40	40
(b) Chillis	3	175
5. Vegetable Crops		
(a) Potato	40	12
(b) Pyaj	20	25
(c) Mahua	40 Per tree	40

Equipments

It is hoped that every cultivator would have a minimum of agricultural tools and equipments of his own, but, unfortunately, this is not so. The well-to-do families are definitely in possesion of almost all important tools and implements, but those that are poor manage their work by borrowing them from others or paying the necessary chareges especially for the plough. Among the indispensable tools which must be kept by each family or cultivators are axe, spade, khurpa, plough, chowkisikar, swing-basket, etc. The axe is used for removing useless plants and cutting woods, spade for digging the soil, khurpa for weeding out useless grass, the sickle for reaping paddy and wheat plants, plough for cultivating land, chowkisikar for mixing seeds in the soil and swing-basket for lifting water from the ditch or pond.

There are 285 wooden ploughs and an equal number of chowkisikars and only one steel plough in the village. The block development office has hired the steel plough on instalment basis to a progressive cultivator in the village. At times such cultivators receive it from the block free of cost. The wooden ploughs are locally made, i.e., by the village carpenters and are cheaper than the steel ploughs, as the former costs simply between Rs. 18/- to 20/- per plough. The steel plough, besides being costly due its usefulness even in dry season, is heavier to which strong bullocks can only be yoked.

There are 49 bullock carts, all made of wood including the wheels. Of these, 34 belong to the Yadavas, 5 each to the Brahmin and Surhi and the rest to other castes. Carts are not so much indispensable for every agriculturists as the bullocks are, because even one cart can serve several families. Generally, owning carts by well-to-do families accrues to their social prestige, but for the poor people it means a source of earning income for the family. Mostly, carts ars used for carrying soil, compost, foddar, etc; and for unloading sacks of grain in the weekly market and elsewhere too. Occasionally, people make use of the cart as a conveyance for going from one place to another, though most of the journeys are undertaken by readily available buses.

Lathakuri, moat and sainkari are used in wet cultivation. A lathakuri consists of a bamboo placed on two fixed wooden poles of which one end is made heavier with few bricks and some mud tied to it, while the other end contains a long rope and an iron vessel fastened to it for lifting up water. When the rope is pulled down the vessel tied to the other end of the rope goes down into the well and when it is left the vessel filled with water comes out and pours water into the field. The moat consists of a long rope and a big leather bag placed on two fixed poles near the well which is drawn by an ox.

The village has two power-driven sugarcane crusher, of which one belongs to a Choudhary and the other to a Surhi. Besides, iron sugarcane crusher is often brought jointly by a few farmers on hire for Rs. 100/- to 150/- from a stockist at Amarpur. In addition, there are 8 chaff cutters, 4 belonging to the Yadavas, 3 to the Brahmins and one to a Surhi.

Method

It has already been mentioned that the agricultural season consists mainly of Kharif and Rabi crops. Agricultural operations in the village are still carried on by the old method of a plough and oxen. Preparations for the sowing of Kharif crops start from the month of Chaitra and the entire process is over by Jyestha. Sowing for the Rabi crops begins from Kartika and is over by the month of Pausha. Paddy seeds are broadcast in a small piece of land and after three ploughings, transplantation work begins in the rainy season when sufficient water gets accumulated in the field. For wheat, barley, maize, gram etc; one to two ploughings ar required immediately after a little shower. Sowing of crops begins according to the Hindu Calender though natural factors are also taken into account. Prof. Lewis (1958:38) describes the method in these words :—

> "In all types of ploughing yoke of standard size is used, and the oxen walk on either side of the furrow, with the plough-

men following behind and keeping to the left of the furrow."5

The first step in harvesting is to cut the plants and to make them into bundles which are carried away in cartloads. Corn stalks are removed from the stems, which are set aside for cattle. This is, perhaps, true to the whole of the countryside. When the ground is moistened, the method of broadcasting seeds is used; but when it is dry, the method of pouring (chhutki) them all along the furrow by a man or woman following behind the ploughman is used. Chowkisikar is yokad to the plough and the ploughman, standing on it, drives the oxen till the seeds are fully covered under or mixed with the soil.

Some astrological or superstitious beliefs also guide farming operations in the village. The priest. after consulting his almanac fixes an auspicious day for sowing seeds and plants. Some rituals are also performed on this occasion. The ground is kept ready in advance and seeds are sown only on the auspicious day. The Muslims and the Untouchables do not consult the priests, but this does not affect the time schedule during which everybody must start sowing. Thursday and Saturday are considered inauspicious, hence sowing is not done on these days. Likewise, Bhadwa, Chaturdashi and Pariwa are inauspicious for any kind of agricultural operation. The plantation work is done mostly by tribal men and women living in the adjacent villages. From morning till night cultivators remain busy with supervising the entire work. The head of the family observes fast on the first day and offers sacrifices of pigeon to the village Gosai (God). Fresh milk is poured on the image of Lord Shiva enshrined in the local Shivalaya and a little quantity of it is poured in the paddy field also to appease the Sun-god. Brahmins are served with Khir (a preparation of cooked rice mixed in milk and sugar) and the women labourers. who come all the way singing to the houses of their employers, are also given food besides their wages.

Animals and cattle

The importance of cattle and other domesticated animals in the agricultural economy and the day-to-day life of the villagers is very great. Perhaps, their utility for ploughing and manuring is greater than lifting water-loads through the moat for purposes of irrigation, grinding mustard in the Kolhu for oil and drawing carts. Oxen and buffaloes (Kara) are the prerequisites for ploughing fields, an old and indigenous method still largely followed in farming. Indeed, agriculture, for its successful operation, depends heavily on these animals and cattle.

Livestock contributes towards a part of the national wealth and, as such, they are deemed as the wealth of the nation. Besides, the number of cows, oxen and buffaloes possessed by an agriculturist helps to determine his socio-economic status in the village. The big and small cultivators are easily distinguished by the number of cattle possessed by them. The larger the number of oxen and buffaloes at the door of an individual, the higher is his status in the village.

Dung, procured from these animals and cattle, is increasingly used as manure and fuel. In course of direct interrogation, it has been found that the villagers commonly believe that compost is in no way inferior to modern fertilizers and chemicals. Women prepare dung-cakes which are seen invariably placed on the roofs or postered on the walls of the dwelling houses. Everywhere in the village, women are busy making piles of such cakes in front of their houses which provide a common sight to the visitors.

Cows and buffaloes are kept for milk and Ghee (butter), the he-goat for its meat and she-goat for children's milk, poultry for personal consumption of eggs and chicken, pigeon and pig for sale as well as for personal consumption. Bharko's total population of animals and cattle is as follows :

Cows including heifer	—	371
Oxen	—	403
He-buffaloes (Kara)	—	99
She-buffaloes	—	660
He-goat	—	73

The goat	—	236
Pig	—	30
Horse	—	4 and
Chicken	—	48

There is only one Hariyana bull which the village has received from the Community Development Block at Amarpur. These figures are presented below in a tabular form :—

Table No. 2.

ANIMALS AND CATTLE AT BHARKO

Types of Animal.		*Number.*
COW (Above 3 Years)		
Milch	—	104
Dry	—	87
HEIFER (Below 3 years)		
he-calf	—	93
she-calf	—	87
OXEN	—	403
BUFFALOES (Above 3 years)		
Milch	—	69
Dry	—	55
He-buffaloes (below 3 years)	—	99
she-buffaloes	—	60
		Total : 1117

Goats :

Goat	*Below 1 year*	*Above 1 year*	*Total*
Male	54	19	73
Female	89	147	236
Total	143	166	309

*Table No. 3**

Type of Milk	*Total Quantity Procured*	*Quantity Consumed*	*Quantity Sold*
Cow's Milk	205 KG	155 KG	50 KG
Buffalo's Milk	42 KG	8 KG	34 KG
Egg — —	132	102	30

The price of cattle in the village is exorbitant and, consequently, cultivators, except the economically better off, cannot afford to keep them. Cultivators of small holdings, landless labourers and untouchables do not keep any cattle at their doors. The price of a Kara in the village is Rs. 300/-. This is perhaps, the greatest handicap of the villagers in their economic prosperity. On the other hand, this causes a set back to agricultural production in the country to a great extent.

Land Ownership

Statistics on land ownership presents a gloomy and disquieting picture so far as the down-trodden and untouchable castes are concerned. In fact, the Yadavas and Surhis belong to the category of backward caste, but their socio-economic status, compared to other castes except the Brahmin, is much higher in the village. The village has practically three land owing castes—namely—Yadava, Brahmin and Surhi and the rest either have meagre amount of land or no land at all.

Land is much valued at Bharko and as such there is a great demand for agricultural land. It is a coveted possession which is instrumental to one's rise in his socio-economic status regardless of his caste in the village community. The following table indicates the distribution of landownership among various castes :

*These figures are based on the report of the All India Cattle Census, 1966.

Table No. 4.

Caste	Total No. of families	Landownership in Bighas	Percentage of landownership
1. Yadava	105	2078	63.3
2. Brahmin	39	660	20.1
3. Baniya	9	12	0.36
4. Kamar	3	7	0.21
5. Halwai	3	13	0.4
6. Kumhar	11	7	0.21
7. Lohar	1	—	Nil
8. Sonar	2	10	0.33
9. Nai	12	16	0.5
10. Dhanuk	29	37	1.12
11. Gorhi	6	26	0.79
12. Laheri	1	1	0.03
13. Surhi	50	300	9.1
14. Teli	1	1	0.03
15. Beldar	23	17	0.51
16. Julaha	22	16	0.5
17. Dhobi	12	10	0.33
18. Chamar	61	30	0.91
19. Dusadh	6	4	0.12
20. Hari	2	3	0.09
21. Rarhi	1	—	Nil
22. Kharadi	35	32	1.0
Total	434	3280	100

In the above table, the highest score is of the Yadavas even when compared to the Brahmins and the Surhis who, relatively, occupy the second and third positions. It is, therefore, evident that, in addition to their numerical strength, the Yadavas exercise overwhelming dominance in the sphere of land ownership also.

On an average, each family of the Yadavas possesses nearly 20 Bighas of land and this is much higher than what is obtainable in the families of other castes. These castes, as shown in the table, possess meagre amount of land. Ownership of land among the untouchables is practically nil.

Size of Landholding

The following table indicates the size of landholding by caste and number of families in the village :

These fiigures unquestionably prove the supremacy of the Yadavas as one family of this caste only and of no other caste, holds land between I00-150 Bighas. The position of the Brahmin is, no doubt, second as one family of this caste also possesses land between 91-100 bighas.

Most of the other castes own land between 1-10 Bighas and this establishes also that the number of poor and landless families in the village is excedingly large.

Table No. 5.

SIZE OF LANDHOLDING BY CASTE & NUMBER OF FAMILIES AT BHARKO.

Size of landhol-ding in Bighas.	*Yadav*	*Brah-min*	*Surhi*	*Kha-radi*	*Cha-mar*	*Bel-dar*	*Jula-ha*	*Dha-nuk*	*Nai*	*Others*
1-10	51	17	21	4	5	5	2	5	4	11
11-20	4	6	2	—	—	—	—	—	—	—
21-30	3	8	3	—	—	—	—	—	—	—
31-40	1	—	1	—	—	—	—	—	—	—
41-50	4	—	3	—	—	—	—	—	—	—
51-60	3	—	1	—	—	—	—	—	—	—
61-70	—	—	—	—	—	—	—	—	—	—
71-80	1	2	—	—	—	—	—	—	—	—
81-90	1	—	—	—	—	—	—	—	—	—
91-100	2	1	—	—	—	—	—	—	—	—
101-150	1	—	—	—	—	—	—	—	—	—
Total	71	34	31	4	5	5	2	5	4	11

Occupational Characteristics

Agriculture constitutes the very core of different economic occupations pursued in the village. In a large measure it is the main source of livelihood for the people, irrespective of whether they do or do not have land. The link beween agricultural occupation and other economic activities is inseparable. The total number of families and persons depending on agriculture and other subsidiary occupations as their main source of livelihood is presented below in a tabular form :

NUMBER OF FAMILIES & PERSONS DEPENDING ON AGRICULTURE FOR THEIR LIVELIHOOD AT BHARKO.

Type of Agricultural workers.	*Total number of families.*	*Total no. of persons*	*Men*	*Women*	*Children*	*No. of persons actually working*	*% of actual workers*
Type of Agriculturist depending on the cultivation of their land	135	831	325	211	295	250	30
Partly agriculturist & partly Agri. worker.	210	1105	300	405	400	815	73.7
Partly agriculturits and partly depending on other crafts and professions.	89	372	118	100	154	200	53.7
Total	434	2308	743	716	849	1265	

The table above shows the highest percentage score, i.e., 73.7% of partly agriculturists and partly agricultural workers. Out of 434 families in the village, a total of 210 families support themselves through these professions. Hence it is easily established that the number of agricultural workers who partly depend on the cultivatian of land is quite large in the village.

Families which depend entirely on the cultivation of land and those that depend partly on agriculture and partly on other crafts and professions occupy the second and third positions respectively. Wherever land is concentrated in a few families or castes, the number of poor or landless families is bound to be great.

Owing to the weekly market, the number of persons specialized in certain crafts and professions has improved very recently.

The occupation wise braekup of the families in the village is shown in the following table :

Type of occupation	No. of families.	Percentage
Agriculturists	135	31.11
Service-holders	29	6.68
Labourers	143	32.95
Traders	44	10.14
Milksellers	5	1.15
Priests	5	1.15
Carpenters	2	0.46
Confectioner	1	0.23
Betelseller	1	0.23
Potters	10	2.30
Blacksmith	1	0.23
Goldsmith	1	0.23

Barbers	5	1.15
Servants	2	0.46
Fishermen	2	0.46
Bangle makers	1	0.23
Weavers	10	2.30
Washermen	10	2.30
Shoemakers	5	1.15
Scavengers	2	0.46
Toy makers	20	4.61
Total	434	

The table presented shows the number of labourers' families as fairly large and, at the same time it shows the number of the families of service-holders and traders as quite encouraging. This helps to infer that the people are now tending to be absorbed largely in service and trade that may he available to them with in and without the village. The table also indicates that the tendency of the people towards caste occupation almost dwindles and the fact of caste remaining today unidentified by its traditional occupation gets established.

Monthly Outside Income

The village derives its income from various other sources besides agriculture. It sends and brings goods and articles to and from the city through its famous weekly market. Exchange of goods and services between the village and the world outside has become a common feature of life in the countryside. On the basis of the types of occupation presented earlier in a table impressions can easily be gathered about the sources of outside income to the families in the village. However, the actual amount of outside income derived from service, busines and several other subsidiary occupations by the families and castes in the village is evident from illustration in the following table :—

AVERAGE MONTHLY OUTSIDE INCOME
BY CASTE & NO. OF FAMILIES.

Caste	*Total of famileis*	*No. of families without side income*	*Average monthly income per family*	*Total outside income.*
1. Yadava	105	15	144.00	2160.00
2. Brahmin	39	17	154,00	2464.00
3. Baniya	9	5	88.00	440.00
4. Kamar	3	3	195.00	585.00
5. Halwai	3	3	78.00	234.00
6. Kumhar	11	8	51.00	408,00
7. Lohar	1	1	75.00	75.00
8. Sonar	2	1	20.00	20.00
9. Nai	12	4	46.00	215.00
10. Dhanuk	29	8	100.00	800.00
11. Gorhi	6	4	128.00	511,00
12. Laheri	1	1	100.00	100.00
13. Surhi	50	19	84.00	1595.00
14. Teli	1	1	120.00	120.00
15. Beldar	23	20	75.00	1500.00
16. Julaha	22	6	67.00	400.00
17. Dhobi	12	2	45.00	90.00
18. Chamar	61	30	66.00	2000.00
19. Dusadh	6	2	25.00	50.00
20. Hari	2	2	63.00	125.00
21. Rarhi	1	1	25.00	25.00
22. Kharadi	35	15	109.00	1635.00
Total	434	168	1858.00	15552.00

The monthly outside income per individual comes to R. 90.50 paise.

Levels of Living

The four broad categories into which the population of the village has been divided are namely, rich, well-to-do, average and poor. The basis selected for these categories is mainly land. Those who possess land between 80-250 Bighas are rich whereas those who have it between 20-50 are known as well-to-do. Similarly, persons or families possessing 1-20 Bighas of land find themselves in the category of average whereas the rest between 0-1 Bigha are under the category of the poor. The percentage of these four categories of people is presented in the follwoing table :

Categories	*Yadava*	*Brahmin*	*Surhi*	*Other*
Rich	13%	8%	8%	—
Well-to-do	8%	21%	8%	—
Average	50%	56%	48%	15%
Poor	29%	15%	38%	85%

Fishing and Other Economic Occupations

At Bharko, fishing, as a traditional occupation, is pursued principally by one caste, i. e., the Gorhi. Undoubtedly, a few Beldar families continue to remain in this occupation, but it is, rather, their subsidiary occupation. The village has seven tanks and a handsome representation of families of fishermen, still no sincere effort seems to have ever been made towards the development of this economic pursuit. It is very recently that the Government has paid a little attention to its development. The establishment of a Fishermen's Cooperative Society with forty four members is the outcome of such encouragement. The block development office has supplid fish-fry to the society for the development of pisciculture. Two tanks have been selected for this purpose on an experimental basis but without any tangible results.

Similarly, an Oilman cooperative Society has been set up for the entire village including its two hamlets. As there is only one family of the Teli, most of the Society members are from the neighbouring villages. Teli sells vegetable oil which is his caste occupation, through an indigenous process of putting oil seeds in the container (Ghani) kept fixed in the ground. A perpendicular roller made of wood for the purpose of grinding is kept in the container which revolves when an ox yoked to the roller starts continuously moving around.

Some crafts like toy-making, rope making and weaving are other economic pursuits followed by some families in the village. While rope making is a pastime job of most of the families, toy-making and weaving are the specialized occupations of the Muslims and Julahas. As has been said earlier, there are 35 families of Muslims who do not own any land but maintain themselves by making toys, chess balls, sticks and other goods, all made up of wood. These goods are sold outside, in towns and cities including Calcutta. Weaving may not be considered as a significant occupation of the Julahas as they are too poor to own any loan. Out of 22 families of the Julahas only two are engaged in this occupation whereas the rest remain absorbed as landless labourers or workers.

REFERENCES

CHAPTER V

1. Bailey F.G., 1958, *Caste and the Economic Frontier,* Quoted by M. N. Srinivas in *Social Change in Modern India,* (Allied Publishers Pvt. Ltd; Bombay).

2. Bailey, F.G., 1955, *An Oriya Hill Village : II, India's Villages,* Development Department, (West Bengal Government Press, Calcutta).

3. Srinivas, M.N., 1966, *Social Change in Modern India,* (Allied Publishers Pvt. Ltd; Bombay).

4. Mayer, A.C., 1952, *Land And Society in Malabar,* (Oxford University Press, Apollo Bunder, Bombay).

5. Lewis, Oscar, 1958, *Village Life in Northern India,* (University of Illinois Press, Urbana, U.S.A).

CHAPTER VI

The Family

The Family

Among groups and institutions the family by far occupies the most important place. It is held as a 'small social system, or a 'natural unit of a society'. A study of the family, therefore, is the immediate concern of a researcher interested in studying the social structure of a community. Stressing the significance of studying a family, Oscar Lewis (1962:3) thus discovers :

> "In studying culture through the intensive analysis of specific families we learn what institutions mean to individuals. It helps us to get beyond form and structure to the realities of human life, or, to use Malinowski's terms (1922:7), it puts flesh and blood on the skeleton. Whole family studies bridge the gap between the conceptual extremes of culture at one pole and the individual at the other. We see both culture and personality as they are interrelated in real life".[1]

Likewise, a study of the family in an Indian village community has its unique importance, particularly when the family is deeply imbedded in the socio-cultural milieu and religious background of the whole Hindu society. In India, the influence of religion and culture on the continuance of joint-living in some form or the other is still very powerful and great.

The Joint Family

Despite the passage of time and the charges it has undergone, the joint family, in some form or the other, continues to exist as a basic social system carrying forward the processes of socialization and cultural continuance. Analysing its role in the maintenance of cultural traditions K.M. Kapadia (1958:246) observes thus :

> "Family tradition was valued above everything, and the primary duty of the head of the family was to ensure that family traditions in all matter relating to life were perpetuated by their solemn observance, however, unmeaningful they might begin to appear as conditions changed. The traditional authority of the head over the junior members of the family was so awe-inspiring that the juniors never thought of expressing their differences, whatever their convictions might be. The subordination and superordination designed to regulate the lives of the different members in the hierarchy of the joint household, recognition of the family as a unit for all social relationships, the place assigned to the family as a juridical unit in family querrels—all tended to give he family such enormous influence that the individual lost his identity in it."[2]

Though it has changed its form and structure still it has retained its substance which can visibly be seen if not in towns, at least in villages in India.

The joint family in India is as old as the Hindu society. Describing its existence in the early periods of the Hindu society, Mrs. Irawati Karve (1965:8) observes :

> "In India the family has endured for as long as any records exist. Even about 1000 B.C., in the time of the Mahabharata war, the joint family existed more or less as it exists today. Earlier records of the Sanskrit texts called Brahmanas and Vedas justify the inference that the patrilineal, patrilocal joint family was in existence even then. Neither the Muslim nor the British rule was able

to modyfy the structure of this most ancient institution of India."[3]

However, as against its huge shape and massive form in the past, the system exists today in its immensely reduced shape and modified form, comprising hardly members of three generations, i.e., the parents, their married sons and the grand children. In its legal form, which is more important today, the system exists largely for the regulation of partition and inheritance. For the most part it is the elementary family which constitutes the family type today in India.

Further, Mrs. Karve (1965:8) defines the system in the following words :

> "A joint family is a group of people who generally live under one roof, who eat food cooked in one kitchen, who hold property in common, participate in common worship and are related to one another as some particular type of kindred."[4]

Except the emphasis 'who generally live and eat together', this definition applies correctly to the existing joint families in both the rural and the urban parts of the country.

Compared to the urban dwellers, people in the countryside are attached in a large measure to the ties of kinship and to their vicinal association. These factors still contribute in some from or the other to the existence of joint family system for the old and the handicapped in the rural areas. Mrs. Gowda (1959 : 465 : 466) describes its usefulness in these words—

> "Hindu joint family system, especially in Rural India, has given a kind of socialism to a very great number of groups constituting joint families with great number of people in each of them. And also the Hindu joint family system in effect has been a kind of insurance against old age and employment. The joint family is there to love, shelter and give food to the unemployed brothers. The grown-up sons are there, who feel it a sacred and bounden duty to respect, love, tend and care for the old parents".[5]

Though in the above paragraph emphasis has been laid on the economic function only, the joint family, besides economic functions, fulfils many more obligations, such as social, cultural, educational, ethical and ritual. Obedience to the parents with out questioning their acts of omissions and commissions is regarded as Dharma. Equally, there should be a harmonious or cordial relationship among brothers, sisters, sons and daughters, besides husband and wife, in a joint family.

Marriage is held still as a sacrament by most of the Hindus and as essential both for the perpetuation of one's family and for his salvation. A son is preferred to a daughter because it is he who performs the death rites and offers oblation to the dead ancestors for their souls to rest in peace. Besides, a son is supposed to take the burden and responsibility of unmarried brothers and sisters as well as of other dependents. Thus, both marriage and family are considered by the villagers as essential for all individuals. Professor S. C. Dube (1955:132) illustrates this fact thus :

> "To the village people the necessity of both marriage and family is self-evident. It is necessary that the family line should be continued. A male heir must be left. An unmarried person past the marriage age is an object of pity. A couple without a son are unhappy. Childlessness and inability to produce a male child on the part of a woman often lead to a polygynous house-hold."[6]

At Bharko the joint family still largely characterises the family type, though its structure has completely changed. The type of joint family found in the village consists mainly of the following members :

Ego : Wife

Unmarried brother | Unmarried sisters

Sons & their Wives | Unmarried daughters

Grandchildren

The concept has been used in this thesis to indicate only the above mentioned members. The following table now shows the distribution of family patterns by caste at Bharko :

DISTRIBUTION OF FAMILY TYPES BY CASTE.

Type of family	*Brahmin*	*Yadava*	*Surhi*	*Harijan*	*Kharadi*	*Others*	*Total*	*Percentage.*
Nuclear or Elementary Family	17	22	10	28	18	52	147	33.8
Extended or Joint Family	21	77	36	30	10	88	262	60.3
Alone	1	6	4	5	7	2	25	5.7
Total	39	105	50	63	35	142	434	100

Undoubtedly, the joint family dominates the family type in the village but in the daily life of the villagers and for all practical purposes it is the elementary or the nuclear family which is more important. Enquiries from the heads of the families reveal that owing to several difficulties most of the members, except the elderly ones, favour the discontinuance of the system. The tempo of increase in the number of the nuclear family leaves no room for any doubt about the villager's preferences for the elementary family and also hints at a major change in the structure of family in the village.

The tendency among the married sons to separate from their parents is quite common. Separation among brothers after marriage is almost proverbial. Among members of the higher castes the tendency to remain in the joint family is greater than what it is among members of the lower castes. Variations in the number of members constituting joint families are due to caste hierarchy and local traditions. Thus, the more a caste is superior, the larger is the size of the household, the more it is inferior, the smaller is the size of the household.

The size of family by caste is presented in the following table :—

SIZE OF FAMILY BY CASTE AT BHARKO.

Size	*Brahmin*	*Yadava*	*Surhi*	*Baniya*	*Chamar*	*Beldar*	*Dhobi*	*Kamar*	*Nai*	*Gorhi*	*Dhanuk*	*Kharadi*	*Others.*
1	2	3	4	5	6	7	8	9	10	11	12	13	14
1-3	11	28	10	4	21	6	6	—	6	2	4	13	20
4-5	16	50	18	2	31	8	6	2	5	2	14	14	22
7-9	8	18	14	2	9	7	—	1	1	2	8	8	5
10-12	1	4	6	1	—	2	—	—	—	—	3	—	1
13-15	2	1	2	—	—	—	—	—	—	—	—	—	—
16-18	2	2	—	—	—	—	—	—	—	—	—	—	—
19-21	—	—	—	—	—	—	—	—	—	—	—	—	—
22-24	—	—	—	—	—	—	—	—	—	—	—	—	—
25-27	—	2	—	—	—	—	—	—	—	—	—	—	—

In the above table families of the Yadava and the Brahmin castes compared to those of other castes, have large nnmber of members. Perhaps, this indicates to their greater disposition to joint living. In other words, it means that the size of the family in the upper castes is comparatively bigger than that in the lower castes. Also, the table shows that the number of elementary families is increasing at a very fast rate.

It is rather difficult to describe the family structure in each of the 22 castes except in each of the three socio-economic layers, viz; upper, middle and lower for purposes of comparison. Caste variations, local traditions and standards of behaviour of the members cause differences in the composition of family in the rural society. However, a comparison between families of different castes in the village is possible if the issue is taken up in relation to the three existing layers.

Certain castes like Beldar, Julaha, Dhobi. Chamar, Dusadh and Hari, which occupy the inferior social and economic status in the village, do not maintain the ideal standards and norms of the family. The harmonious relationship and corporate unity which prevail among members of the upper castes are conspicuously absent in the lower or the untouchable castes. These norms and ideals find accord in principle from all the castes including even the Kharadis who are the Muslims, but in actual practice they are not enforced by the lower and the untouchable castes. Normally, members of these castes do not have any respect for age or the superior kinship-status of their members. Invariably, sons have separated from their fathers just after two years of their marriage. Frequent quarrels between the sons and their fathers, nephews and their uncles helped by other members of the kin who may be inferior in age and kinship position, are widespread among them. Desertion of the old and the incapacitated parents by their sons, divorce or separation between husband and wife, maltreatment to women and children are the common features of the families belonging to these castes.

Men are generally supposed to work outside and women to remain at home. The responsibility of running the family rests with the male members and the female members are not supposed to share the economic burden of the family. This is, however, not applicable to those women of the lower and untouchable castes who have either children or who bear somewhat aged look. Some of the remunerative jobs, which are done exclusively by women and for which payments are made either in cash or kind, include paddy plantation, removal of paddy from its stem, preparation of rice and Chura (chipped rice) and harvesting of Chaita crops. Except those who find it difficult to manage the family with the small income of their husbands and thus work as casual labourers, none else breaks through the household confinement. The villagers live under the notion that women are basically meant for taking care of their husbands, for the upbringing of their children and not for doing outdoor work.

As only the patriarchal type characterises the family in the village, the importance of father as the head of the family is great. Among the lower and untouchable castes father continues to occupy this position until the sons have become the earning members or have separated from him after about two years of their marriage. Those married brothers, who still share the same house along with their wives and children, prepare meals separately. It is only on ceremonial occasions that the separate units of the family join together. In certain cases the son-in-law after the death of the father-in-law, lives with his mother-in-law but it does not constitute a case of matrilocal residence. Often, this is necessitated due to the economic hardship of the mother-in-law or in some cases, due to nonconformity with the ideals of the family. According to the prevailing norms neither the son-in-law is supposed to reside with his mother-in-law nor the mother-in-law with her son-in-law in each other's house. Similarly, the parents of the son-in-law should in no circumstance reside with the parents of the daughter-in-law and vice-verse. Failure to do so results in severe social criticisms. The upper but not the lower and the untouchable castes live up to these edials.

Though the Yadavas belong to the categoly of the lower or the backward caste, yet in the caste hierarchy of the village they rank next to the Brahmins. The important traits of the family of this particular caste are briefly outlined here. On the basis of the maintenance of family norms and good conduct, the Yadavas like other castes may be grouped into the upper, the middle and the lower ones. The Choudharies belong to the upper strata, the Mahtos to the middle and the Manjhis and others to the lower strata in the village. Apart from exercising a preponderating influence on the socio-economic and political life of the village, the Choudharies have Sanskritized themselves to the extent that a similarity in respect of standards of behaviour and good conduct exists between them and the Brahmins. Mutual understnding. cooperative undertakings, friendly treatment, generosity, respect for age and superior kinship status, observanee of traditions and norms of the family, maintenance of prestige and cultural distintiveness are the dominant traits of the village. Dissenssion and discord, tension and conflict even on slight provocations which occur among brothers and near kins of the Mahtos and the Manjhis, do not figure in the interpersonal relationships of the Choudharies.

It is the father who acts as the head of the family and exercises traditional authority and control over the members of the family. Members of the family respect him and honour his decisions without any reservation. After he has grown pretty old and physically invalid, he delegates the power to his eldest son who subsequently manages the affairs of the family. When the father is dead, the mother assumes this responsibility till the sons attain their adulthood. Women observe Purdah and are, therefore, not seen outside the four walls of their houses except on ceremonial occasions. Not even a single case of divorce or remarriage has so far been heard in any of the Choudhary families and as far as possible members of the nuclear families tend to remain united for a long time.

The aforesaid qualities do not completely nullify the presence of certain negative traits of the joint family among the Choudharies. Quarrels between brothers or their wives and even among children often lead to snapping of all brotherly ties and finally to separation from the joint family. Today, spilt in the joint family or demand for partition of the common property engineered due to jealousy and conflict between brothers is more pronounced than what it was in the past. However, unlike the families of the Mahtos and the Manjhis, who are the Bhaginmans (son-in-laws), there is not even a single instance of the sons in a Choudhary family having ever demanded separation or partition during the life time of their father. In the day-to-day life the nuclear families remain free from the interference or control of the joint family; nevertheless, each of them maintains formal contacts with the heads of the joint and allied families, though inwardly both strive for each other's troubles and miseries. Except on ceremonial occasions like marriage and death when these units of the joint families get temporarily united and act (for fear of social criticism) in mutual cooperation and on advice from the seniors, they remain, in everyday life, unconcerned about the affairs of the other. This is certainly a major development which has, today, largely affected the structure and organization of the family in the Indian countryside. Politics and other disruptive forces within the joint family have led to increased separatist tendencies among the members, the consequnce of which is the largescale modern individual or unitary families.

The Muslims, who differ from the Hindus in socio-cultural religious matters, maintain quite different standards and norms in respect of family and marriage. Unlike the Hindus, the conception of an ethical or ideal joint family system and of a sacramental nature of the marriage system is preeminently absent among the Muslims. Besides, striking dissimilarities in the patterns of organization and function of these social institutions exist between them.

Relationship within the Family

In a joint family, every member, according to his or her kinship status, works ceaselessly towards strengthening its unity and solidarity. Father is the head (Mukhiya) of the family and is the authoritarian figure traditionally exercising absolute control over the household management. In this respect his responsibility is great as he should be just and impartial in his dealings with all the members who should equally cooperate with him in running the family. The joint family system promises several benefits to the members, particularly to those who are physically handicapped or are unemployed. But in the present age when conditions are entirely changed making the joint family quite untenable and weak, it is the unitary family which the villagers regard as very advantageous to them.

Relationship between Husband and Wife

In the interpersonal relationships of members within the family, the relationship between husband and wife occupies the most significant place. Tradition assigns the husband a position superior to that of his wife in an Indian family. This is no longer the case in the urban society though it is still so in the rural society of the country. For unity and solidarity of the family, villagers favour a dominating husband and a docile wife. The husband is thought to be his wife's lord entitled to receive sincere service and devotional care from her, irrespective of his good or bad qualities. The husband is his wife's treasure because among the Brahmins and the Yadavas divorce and widow marriage are still considered as against social tradition. Unlike the case of women in Jaunsar-Bawar studied by Professor R.N. Saxena (1962 :29), divorce and widow marriage are not practised by the upper castes in the village.[7] If it is the husband's responsibilty to meet all his wife's and children's needs or requirements, it is equally the wife's duty to manage the household and keep it in order. Besides having sense of neatness and cleanliness, a good wife should also be good natured, serviceable, tolerant and well-versed in domestic affairs. The wife must not be illtempered, uncompromising, spendthrift and careless which are regarded as bad qualities.

It is the husband who provides subsistence to his wife and children, though in the lower and untouchable castes the wife also contributes something towards her maintenance. Of course, this happens in cases where couples run independent or separate households and are unable to meat their pressing economic needs. After a particular age, neither the husband nor the wife interferes in each other's work and household problems are mostly mutually solved.

The sons start their conjugal life while living with the parents; hence the amount of freedom enjoyed in a separate household or after a particular age is perhaps curtailed. The bride does not face her husband before the senior members of the family and both get together only at night when everybody is asleep. For a month she is not given to prepare food. She remains under the direct control of her mother-in-law. She endeavours to be more serviceable and obedient to her than to her husband because she is always conscious that displeasure of her mother-in-law would mean her husband's displeasure or dislike even. This sort of thing characterises the earliest phase in the married life and it changes only in course of time.

Relationship Between Parents and Children

The father provides support and maintenance and the mother care to the children till they are able to earn their own living. It is equally the duty of the children to remain obedient and subservient to their parents and to take their sole care when they are old and invalid. In addition, it is the duty of the parents to correct their children if they do any wrong. The amount of punishment given to them by their parents is usually measured by the intensity of wrong doings. They fear their mother less than their father who exercises stringent control over them. Describing the parent and child relationship among the Pandits of Utrassu-Umanagari, T.N.Madan (1965 : 99) discovers this fact —

> "The Pandit boys do not develop the kind of intimacy with their parents which the daughters do. A son also is, however, freer with his mother than with his father. A mother usually does not scold or exercise authority over a grown-up son; she almost treats him with respect. Sons in their turn usually show greater affection for their mothers than for their fathers."[8]

Children between 5-6 years of age are fondled, loved and even spared for any amount of wrong doings but as soon as they cross that stage, they are put to discipline and made to cultivate ideals of good behaviour and conduct. It is hoped that burden and responsibilty of the family will fall on the sons after their father's death as the daughters join their husbands' families after marriage. Hence the parents remain much concerned about building the future prospect of their children. The parent and child relationship undergoes a change with the skipping over of the different phases of life. The old notion, that fondling should continue till the age of five, beating till ten years and no sooner the sons attain sixteen years of age, they should be treated as friends or equals, is still prevalent in the village.

Their fear of the father reduces gradually with the attainment of youth or adolescence but in no circumstance their love and respect for the father change. Unlike their counterparts in the lower castes, children in the upper castes act mostly according to the prevailing social norms and cultural values. Unless required to do so, they do not generally face him or sit before him even when he is either alone or is engaged in conversation with persons of his age. They equally avoid showing any emotional involvement in their own wives or children before the father.

It forms an important part of the parent's duty to settle the marriages of the sons and daughters. To get a suitable match for one's daughter, whose marriage cannot be postponed after the age of eighteen, is a difficult task. Botherations and anxieties, associated with daughter's marriage, do not accompany son's marriage. As already stated, daughters join their husbands' families immediately after marriage and gradually begin to loose contacts with their parental families where they come to stay only for a few days on some ceremonial occasions. The father, with his son's marriage, begins to change his authoritarian and patriarchal position into an affectionate and compassionate one, though his sons still have the same fear and awe of their father. M.C. Pradhan (1966: 62) describes the relationship between the father and the married sons, equally found in the village under study, in these words :

"The authority of the father within the family is strong. As the head of the family he commands all the economic and other resources belonging to it. Even after their marriage the sons have to obey the father and conform to his wishes. Senior status is not achieved immediately after marriage; it takes from five to seven years before a married person is considered sufficiently grown-up and responsible as a member of the society. Till then he is not considesed independent."[9]

Siblings

The cultural pattern and traditional norm that guide the relationship between the siblings in a joint family find expression in respect, love, submission and obedience shown to each other according to age status. They foster among themselves unstinted cooperation and unity that are necessary for the achievement of their prosperity and well-being. It is the eldest son who mostly runs the family when the father becomes old and invalid and, therefore, he receives respect and regards from all his younger brothers. On the other hand, the eldest accords fatherly treatment and his wife her motherly affection to his junior brothers. Being the seniormost amongst all his brothers, he shares the responsibility of their maintenance, education and marriage and, as far as possible, keeps them united for long even after their marriage. However, after sometime, conflict and split occur between the brothers which eventually lead to their separation. Analysing the new processes of formation and fission in the joint families, that are equally operative in the village under study David G. Mandelbaum (1955 : 13 :14) comes to this fiuding :

"Joint families have long been in a continuous process of formation and fission. As a joint family came to include many nuclear families, and as the main were mainly the sons and grandsons of brother's father than brothers, strains developed which cause such a joint family to divide the common property and split up. The usual reason given for such partition is that the women could not get along together. Thus parted, a man alone or a set of brothers established a new joint family. As their childeren grew to adulthood and their sons married and had children, that joint family might increase to a point where it was of a size conducive to partition and the process would be repeated".[10]

Although at Bharko joint families do not include the father's own brothers as they separated from him with their wives and children immediately after the death of the grandfather, yet the prevailing norm requires thc siblings to accord their uncle and aunt the same respect and honour as are given to the parents and to maintain contacts with them. The uncle and aunt should not also discriminate between their own and the cousin sons and daughters. At times, these children, after their father's death, remain under the care and supervision of their uncle but this is a purely temporary arrangement. Besides the nature of supervision and control exercised by the uncle, it depends upon the amount or degree of cordiality and intimacy.

Today, relationships between the uncle and the nephew or between cousin brothers are mostly characterised as embittered and hostile. However, they all are temporarily and formally united on certain ceremonial occasions like marriage and death.

As the joint families in Bharko have recently taken to a smaller or a more limited size the question of the inclusion of a large number of relatives does not arise. However, grandparents still live in few families, though they practically lead a retired life owing to old age and physical disability. As most of them are unable to do any work they spend their time leisurely in prayers or meditation. Only those who are somewhat physically fit supervise a little of agricultural work like thrashing of paddy and winnowing of wheat, going on in front of their house or keep a watchful eye on cattle and other belongins or receive visitors in absence of their sons. Besides, they spend their time in play and gossip with their grandchildren who are to be kept engaged while their mothers are busy with the domestic work. In some of the well-to-do families the grandparents accopanied by their sons go on pilgrimage to certain holy places in the country.

Other Affinal Kins

Among the affinal kins with whom the family is in constant touch and who pay visits either on some important occasions or when summoned for some urgent work are the maternal uncle, son-in-law and his father. But the attachment with the maternal uncle is comparatively great as he renders all help and support in any critical situation. Internal differences, conflicts and economic hardships of the family are disclosed to him and not to any other relative. The sons and daughters in a Choudhary or a Brahmin family treat their maternal uncle like their father.

REFERENCES

CHAPTER VI

1. Lewis, Oscar, 1962, *Five Families*, (Science Editions, INC, New York).

2. Kapadia, K.M., 1958, *Marriage And Family in India*, (Oxford University Press, Apollo Bunder, Bombay).

3. Karve, Irawati, 1965, *Kinship Organization in India*, (Asia Publishing House, Bombay).

4. *Ibid.*

5. Gowda, L.D.M., 1959, *Wither Rural India*, 37, Krishna Rajendra Road, Basavangudi, P.O. Bangalore-4, India.

6. Dube, S.C., 1955, *Indian Village*, (Routledge & Kegan Paul Ltd., Broadway House, London).

7. Saxena, R.N., 1962, *Social Economy of a Polyandrous People*, (Asia Publishing House, Bombay).

8. Madan, T.N., 1965, *Family And Kinship*, Asia Publishing House, Bombay).

9. Pradhan, M.C., 1966' *The Political System of the Jats of Northern India*, (Oxford University Press, Apollo Bunder, Bombay-1).

10. Mandelbaum, D.G., 1955, '*Social Organization And Planned Culture Change in India*'—India's Villages Development Department, (West Bengal Govt. Press, Calcutta).

CHAPTER VII

Ritual Structure

The influence of religion and rituals on the people of India, or on the whole of the Hindu Society, is still very powerful and great. Religious beliefs and practices are held essentially as supreme in both the city and the country. These beliefs and practices have in fact, upheld the social institutions and provided guidelines for good conduct and better understanding of the members of the community. This shows the interconnection between religion and society. Quite apart from its function of regulating behaviour and shaping ideology, religion acts as a cementing factor for the members of a community and fulfils most of their vital needs. K.S.Mathur (1964 : 78) in his study of caste and rituals in Malwa observes :

> "Religion helps a society integrate and perpetuate its social order in two ways :
>
> (i) it provides a 'Philosophy' to the social system, in the form of doctrine, dogma and myth; and
>
> (ii) the rites, that is, ceremonial actions and ritual prohibitions, dogmatise the social system and transmit from one generation to another sentiments on which the constitution of the society depends."[1]

Hinduism

It is really a difficult task to present a systematic exposition of Hinduism in all its aspects and at all stages of development on account of its complex and amorphous nature. Moreover, reference to Hinduism, as one finds in the religious scriptures, classical and modern text books, is not needed just for describing the religious attitude or behaviour of the people in a village which has a clear majority of the Hindus. The great tradition of Hinduism and the local little tradition marked by a continuous process of Sanskritization identify Bharko with Marriott's Kishan Garhi. This issue would be taken up for discussion on subsequent pages in this chapter.

It is not an exaggeration if all Hindus are said to be essentially religious. Religiosity is pronounced more among the people living in the countryside than among those in a city. The degree of variation tn religiosity is caused due to several factors—individual, caste, creed, sect, community etc. Besides, Hinduism itself is a vast and intricate phenomenon and it can not be delineated, even for the purpose of analysis, into what Dr. M.N. Srinivas (1952 : 213) calls :

> 'All-India Hinduism', 'Peninsular Hinduism', 'Regional Hinduism', and 'Local Hinduism'[2].

It is not the concept of split rather his concept of spread, in both of its aspects—horizontal spread and vertical spread, that furnishes a satisfactory explanation of the process of absorption of religion's great tradition by the little communities in the country.

In the village, Hinduism functions in its vague and crude form, completely devoid of the philosophical and metaphysical profundity of the Upanishads, the Vedanta and the Gita. The purely spiritual of mystical aspect of Hinduism is beyond the comprehension level of the villagers. Instead, its devotional and practical aspect appears to be much more significant. Professor S.C. Dube (1953 : 93) amicably remarks thus :

> "Clearly, Hinduism as it is practised in the village is not the Hinduism of the classical philosophical heights, nor the abstract content of the latter. It is a religion of fasts, feasts and festivals, in which the prescribed rituals cover all the major crises of life. Worship and propitiation of gods and spirits follow the annual round of festivals and

the ritual of human life-cycle. Disease and difficulty may also necessitate invoking assistance from these sources... Analysis of life histories reveals that spiritualism cannot be said to be the key note in the life of the community : far from it, the religion appears to be a practical one."[3]

More or less an identical view on this issue has been expressed by Professor Morris Opler (1950 : 314) who writes :

> "The fact that the highest goal of the Hindu is to eliminate earthly concerns, desires, and personal existence itself introduces a large element of asceticism, intellectualism, detachment, and withdrawal into Hindu religious philosophy."[4]

Hence, it is obvious that Hinduism, for its increasingly ideal and ethical tinge as reflected in the above statement, does not justify its application to the rural masses. It is rather applicable to a good many saints, seers and to those intellectuals who may or may not have faithfully adhered to the ideals of life set out by the four Ashramas. Dr. Radhakrishnan (1961 : 24) thus illustrates :

> "The worshipers of the Absolute are the highest in rank; the second to them are the worshippers of personal God; then come the worshippers of the incarnations like Rama, Krishna, Buddha; below them are those who worship ancestor, deities and sages, and lowest of all are the worshippers of the petty forces and spirits."[5]

Dharma

Certain theological concepts that are purely Sanskritic in nature like Dharma (the way of iife), Karma (action), Swarga (Heaven), Naraka (hell), Pap (sin), Punya (merit), Mokshya (Salvation), etc. are widespread among the people of both sexes as well as among literates and illiterates in the village. The concept of Dharma is used in several senses but that which is fundamental to it is the ethical sense. Its interpretation by a few westerners as an equivalent for religion is not correct. Basically, it stands for the way of life of that which is right or moral. Living unquestionably according to the moral code is Dharma. In its wider connotation, it includes the different phases ol life-cycle and the processes of what Professor Dube calls intragroup and intergroup relations, Adherence to Dharma with all rigidity and orthodoxy is met with reward, and failure to obey it is fraught with punishment here and hereafter. According to Professor Srinivas (1952 : 26), observance of Dharma effects one's birth in a higher caste in his next life with a silver spoon in his mouth and failure to do so accompanies birth in a low caste along with poverty disease and fear of annihilation because Dharma guides destiny. Observance of norms and values, rules of caste, pollution, maintenance of moral character, feelings of compassion for the poor and needy, respect for the sacred literature and prayer or worship are some of the outward expressions of Dharma found among the people of the village. Though a few old and elderly persons still adhere to these prescriptions, yet the young and educated are not at all sincere about observing them. Consequently, a general trend towards decline in the observance of these codes has recently become manifest.

According to the rules of caste-pollution, a Brahmin is supposed to keep himself, while talking, one and a half yards away from a Dusadh and must not accept food or water touched by any unclean or untouchable caste. Even physical contact with a Chamar, Dhobi, Hari and Muslim is prohibitory for Brahmin and a Choudhary. About three years ago a Brahmin, while living in a distant town, married a tribal girl, perhaps a Christian by religion, which resulted in ex-communication of the boy's parents by all the Brahmins of the village. Another case of ex-communication is of a Yadava for performing remarriage (Chumauna) of his daughter.

Water of the Ganga is sacred to all the Hindus in the village and a dip into it is holy. Quite a large number of people belonging to clean castes have been found going to Bhagalpur to take a bath in the Ganges on Maghi Purnima and Kartik Purnima days. The Brahmins and the Yadavas observe fast (Vrata) and undertake pilgrimage to holy places like Deoghar (Baidyanath-Dham), Kashi and Prayag. During Pitripaksha,

Choudharies and Surhis go to Gaya to offer oblation to their dead ancestors.

Karma

Dharma and Karma are the basic concepts in Hindu religion which explain the continuous process of the life-cycle, cultural norms, values, social institutions and social solidarity. Villagers communicated their views thus.

> If you do good action in your present life, you can expect to be born in a high caste in the next life... The simple truth is that the more Punyatama (one who earns spiritual merits) an individual is, the nearer is his soul to God and conversely, the more Papatma (one who earns sin) he is, the distant is his soul from God.

In general, an action according to the moral code is regarded as virtuous. Certain actions like murder, dacoity, gambling. prostitution, accepting wine or addiction to it, adultery, exploitation of the poor, cruelty etc. must not be committed by any one, whatever be his caste. A Brahmin is not supposed to steer a plough in the field and take to any mean profession. T. R. Singh (1966 : 135-36) in his study of ritual purity and pollution in Madhuwaram village suggests certain levels thus—

(a) one degree fall in the situational level;

(b) two degree fall in the situational level;

(c) three degree fall in the situational level;

(d) four degree fall in the situational level, and

(e) five degree fall in the situational level in the analysis of ritual purity and impurity.

These levels can effectively be applied to the study of ritual purity and pollution at Bharko also. Some types of ritual practices observed commonly or individually at Bharko are the following :

1. Relatlng to urination or touching ritually impure objects, sprinkling water over the body or washing hands and feet.

2. Relating to the touch of a person in mourning, a menstruating women or touch of a women in delivery—ritual bath, undergoing for a certain period the process of observing impurity and observing other pollution-removing ceremonies.

3. Relating to eating or drinking of food and water touched by a Sudra—ritual bath, undergoing sin-removing ceremonies, bathing in the Ganges and drinking its water, visiting sacred places and giving feast to the Brahmins.

4. Worshipping deity etc.—ritual bath, observing fast, taking food offered to the deity (Sital Prasad).

5. Relating to marriage—rubbing turmeric paste, decorating eyes with Kajal, ritual bath and worshipping deities.

6. Cooking and eating food—ritual bath, observance of purity by men, women and children.

Hence, besides observance of caste pollution, regular morning bath is obligatory for all the castes from the standpoint of ritual purity. For external purification of the body, particularly after excreting urine, faeces and semen, regular morning bath is essential. The people of the village do not perform worship (Puja) unless they have taken purificatory bath. Both men and women of the Brahmin, Yadava, Baniya, Surhi, Nai and other castes wash hands and feet after urination and, in addition, change their clothes after excreting faeces. Women are more conservative than men in observing ritual pollution. A menstruating woman is impure for three days during which she withdraws herself completely from such activities as preparing food and giving water to the members of her family. The impurity is removed on the fourth day when she goes for a full purificatory bath.

The impact of modern forces has brought about a slight modification in the observance of all the prescriptions of Dharma; nevertheless, these prescriptions still remain fresh in the minds of the people. Everyone belives in the existence of God and the soul. A virtuous man gets Moksha (Salvation) and will not come again on this earth as a being. In that case his soul gets merged with God who is called Parmatma in the local language. Villagers believe in the transmigration or the indestructibility of soul. A person who does good action throughout his life gets heaven (Swarga) after his death and if at all he has to come again as a being, he would be born in a high caste with all the comforts of life. Conversely, the soul of a man, who has done only bad actions (Pap) during his life time, will get hell (Naraka) after his death. A good action is an action in accordance with religious and moral prescriptions. It consists of worship of God, giving feasts and other gifts to the Brahmins, holy bath, pilgrimage to religious places, giving alms to the beggars, etc. On the contrary, a bad action consists of adultery, prostitution, dacoity, murder, torture to and exploitation of the poor. T. R. Singh's analysis of the ritual purity and impurity, still largely prevalent among members of different castes in the rural areas, is very fine and praiseworthy. But the five levels, as suggested by him for using them as an elementary method of measuring the rise and fall in an individual's ritual situation, have yet to be examined in the light of changes due to non-conformity in both the South and the North Indian villages.

Village Pantheon

The distribution of Hindus and Muslims is uneven in the village. Hindus are proportionately larger in number whereas the size of the Muslim population is relatively small. The Muslims constitute a separate entity and are self-sufficient and independent in their religious spheres.

The Hindus are a staunch believer in a plurality of gods and goddesses, reposing, at the same time, their faith in spirits and magic. They are worshippers of a large number of Sanskritic, regional and local deities as well as followers of particular cults. The influence of Shakt Mat—Cult of Durga or Goddess of Strength on the entire village appears to be very powerful. K. N. Sharma (1961 : 47) gives an exposition of the sect of Shaktism in the following words :

> One of the most important doctrines of Shaktism is Tantric one, that passion can be destroyed and exhausted by

passion. Panch Tattva or Five 'Makers' or Five 'M's are foremost features of Tantrism. These Five 'M's are : Wine (Madya), meat (Mansa), fish (Matsya), holy finger gestures (Mudra) and copulation (Maithuna).

The devotional aspect of religion can not exist along with these doctrines which encourage both eating of certain kinds of non-vegetarian food and wine.[8] While the Brahmins (of Maithil sub-caste) and the lower castes have adopted the Shakt Mat, the Yadavas and Surhis are devoted to the Vaishnava and Kabir cults respectively. Every Brahmin family has established a seat (Pindi) of Bhagwati Durga (Goddess of Strength) in a small room of the residential house where worship (Puja) and animal sacrifice (Bali) are offered to the deity uninterruptedly on the Dussahera festival. Hence, Brahmins of the village, who belong to a sub-caste known as Maithil, are non-vegetarian as they are the followers of Shakt Mat, which accepts Bhagwati or Durga as the Supreme Godhead. Dr. Radhakrishnan (1961 : 33) expresses his views about the Goddess thus :

> It is clear that Kali in her various shapes is a non-Aryan Goddess. But she was gradually identified with the supreme Godhead. Despite her identification with the Brahmin in whom all the three conditions of existence become manifest, animal sacrifices continue to be offered to the deity by her devotees everywhere in the country.[9]

In the village, Durga is commonly known as Bhagwati and is considered to be the most powerful among the deities. In this part of the State, only the Maithil Brahmins, but no other Brahmins, and all the lower castes offer sacrifices of goat to the Bhagwati. There is a centrally situated Bhagwati Asthan (platform) for the whole village where approximately 150 goats are sacrificed every year on the Dussahera day by the people of the village and of a few closely situated villages. On the other hand, the Yadavas are the followers of Vaishanava cult known as Radhaswamy Mat of Dayal Bagh, Agra, are, therefore, vegetarians though, today, quite a large number of them, mostly the educated youths and those inferior to the Choudharies, have defected to the so-called ideal of non-vegetarianism. The concept of vertical spread is truly applicable to Bharko as in some degree the Brahmins and Choudharies share the common cultural forms. Dr. Srinivas (1952 : 14) maintains thus :

> A linguistic area is a culturally homogeneous area relatively speaking, and the Brahmins in any linguistic area share some cultural and ritual forms with all other castes, imcluding the lowest, in that area.[10]

Professor Srinivas calls this type of spread, common to all the castes, 'vertical spread'.

The Gosai or gods and goddesses worshipped at Bharko are mainly the following :—

1. Shiva (One of the three Divine Lords, the destroyer) ;
2. Mahabir (Monkey-God);
3. Bhagwati (Goddess of power);
4. Shitala Mai (Goddess of small pox);
5. Kali Mai (Same as Bhagwati);
6. Barmaine (from Brahmin believed to be the spirit of the Brahmin widow) which presides over the destiny of the Choudharies.
7. Danab (Demon-God protecting village boundaries);
8. Yogin (Goddess of spirits and witch-craft);
9. Bhae Haran (Deity removing fear of physical sufferings), and
10. Bishahri (Goddess of snake).

The first five contained in the above list are popular throughout India or of 'All India spread', whereas the rest are local gods and goddesses. In fact, a few among the local, deities are also found in the rural areas of other states, but are known by different names.

Local Shrines

Caste constitutes the structural basis of religion in a village, hence the dominance of the Yadavas has proved to be immanent in the location and erection of Shrines at Bharko. The

Yadavas have a separate temple of their own known as Thakurbari in which images of Lord Krishna and Radha are installed. In addition to this, the village has one Shiva temple known as Shivalaya for its entire people. The image of Mahabir is kept close to the Shivalaya on an elevated platform known as Mahabir Asthan. Both the Shivalaya and the Mahabir Asthan are situated at the entrance of the village where the weekly market is held. Shivalaya, Thakurbari and Bhagwati Asthan are pucca built and centrally located, whereas the rest of the shrines in the village are mudbuilt and situated distantly.

The Barmaine Asthan is sacred to the Choudharies and it is only they who are permitted to enter it. What to speak of the Brahmins, even Yadavas who are not Choudharies are inhibited to visit this place. In the shrine one can see only a hole in the centre of the earth believed to be the seat of the spirit. The hole remains covered with fire pan and basket and thus the entire room presents a dreadful look. The Barmaine is considered more or less as the family deity of the Choudharies which Presides over their welfare. Besides, the Choudharies are also having their separate Kali Asthan, Bhagwati Asthan and Sitala Asthan where people of all other castes, except the Kapri Brahmins, are not permitted to offer prayer or sacrifices. As has been said earlier, the Kapri Brahmins are held to be inferior by other Brahmins of the village for being exclusively the family priests of the Yadavas and for retaining their Kapri surname, believed to have been given by the Yadavas to these Brahmins.

The question of a separate Bhagwati Asthan for the Brahmin does not arise because Bhagwati is their family deity (Gosai) and as such her Pindi is kept in each and every Brahmin family. However, they have one separate Kali Asthan. The Surhis, Baniyas, Halwais, etc. worship in the Shivalaya and Bhagwati Asthan meant for all the people of the village. The untouchable castes—Chamar, Hari, Dhobi and Dusadh offer Puja and sacrifices in the Kali Asthan, which they own jointly though they are also permitted to offer sacrifices in the Bhagwati Asthan meant for the entire village community. Besides, small images of gods and goddesses are kept by the Brahmins, Yadavas and other castes. Those who do not have keep pictures of different gods and goddesses of Sanskritic nature and in that way, the Hindus of the village share much in common with those in the country.

Witchcraft

Quite apart from an unshakable faith in a multiplicity of gods and goddesses of 'all-India-spread', villagers also believe in supernatural powers like ghosts and spirits. The village has a good number of witches and witch-doctors (Bhagat) who are an object of fear to the people. The witches are supposed to be capable of inflicting all types of physical sufferings starting from temporary to a long and continued illness, blood-vomiting and finally to death. In such situations villagers generally take recourse to a witch-doctor and infrequently to a medicine. However, cases of natural illness and disease are invariably referred to the present-day medical practitioners.

During Durga Puja, the witches exercise the powers of their magic to gain maturity by dancing naked at the dead of night in solitary and dreadful places like cross-roads, burning ghats, ponds, etc. They offer daily prayers to the Bhagwati and Kali during the period to get their blessings for the success in their art. Dussahera Puja is also considered as an opportune time for those who want to learn this art. Special care of the children is taken so that they might not fall a prey to the evil eyes of these witches. Earlier it has been mentioned that snakes and scorpions are found in a large number in the village. In every case of a snake-bite, villagers rush to the Ojhas (those who cure cases of snake-bite through Mantras) who have successfully cured several such cases.

Rituals of Birth

Whenever a child is born in a Yadava or a Brahmin family or in the families of other clean castes, the woman is kept in a secluded apartment of the residential house. Though the village has a trained midwife, yet it is the local untrained Hari woman who is called to attend delivery cases. She comes regularly for three days, takes special care of both the mother and the child and even stays with them at night for their comforts. The Hari woman renders several services, such as cutting the child's navel-string, kneading the body of both the mother and the child with oil and washing their dirty clothes. To keep them warm, a fire is kept burning inside the room which is closed to thwart the possibility of an evil eye falling on them. Superstitiously enough, a living scorpion is burnt in the fire believing that the child won't ever feel any pain caused by its sting. Until the pollution-removing ceremony is held, the whole family undergoes impurity for a period of five days. Sufficient indications regarding the birth of a child are given by hanging shells, dung cakes and thorny plants at the entrance of the house and even outside the labour room. Both the mother and the child are regarded as defiling till the observance of Chhatti (Sixth Day Ceremony).

The Chhatti ceremony is usually held on the sixth day of the birth of the child but if the child is under the influence of any bad star, it is observed on the twenty-seventh day called Sataisa. The whole house is fully washed, the floor polished with cowdung and the old earthen pots are replaced by new ones. Both the mother and the child along with all other female members, get their nails cut and they all undergo purificatory bath in the morning. At night, female members worship Chhatti in the Goasi Ghar (room for the family deity) and offer food to the deity. The mother and the child are dressed up in new clothes, and if it is the birth preferably of the first male child, besides the female members of the family, the Hari and the Nai women also receive new clothes. As child-birth is welcomed with joy and happiness, a feast is arranged at which castemen and friends are entertained. It is customary that the father's sister will apply Kajal (dust collected from the flames of an earthen lamp and is used for decorating eyes) is mixed with oil in the eyes of the child for which she receives presents from her brother. The child is then shown to the invitees who shower their blessings and present money or gifts to the child.

Rituals of Marriage

Ceremonial marriage is the widely prevalent form found among the people of the village. Excepting a few young men reading in schools and colleges who are in favour of intercaste marriage, quite a large number of people, belonging to various age and caste groups, still adhere to traditional caste marriages. Recent ex-communication of two families for showing non-conformity to the caste prescriptions indicates the rigidity and rigorousness with which marriage rules are observed by different castes in the village.

Most of the marriages are settled through negotiation. Differences in marriage practices are due to caste variations. For instance, among the Yadavas and Brahmins, it is the parents of the girl who are first required to go to the parents of the boy with the proposal for the marriage of their daughter, whereas among the lower castes it is the parents of the boy who approach the parents of the girl for their son's marriage. Moreover, it is also customary for the Yadavas and Brahmins to finalise their son's marriage without seeing the girl. But this is conversely true of the lower and the exterior castes, as both the boy and the girl must be seen by the parties concerned prior to reaching any final agreement. If for any reason the girl does not suit their choice, final word about marriage is not given and the negotiation is dropped. But if the girl is found suitable or acceptable to the members of the boy's family, a simple ceremony called Cheka or Wakya Dan which signifies engagement is performed on an auspicious day. After the ceremony is over, it now becomes, if not a legal, at least a moral obligation for the boy's parents to marry their son to this particular girl from whose parents they have accepted the Cheka. On this occasion a party consisting of a few members of the girl's family goes to the groom's place where, in the presence of his family members and the priest, he receives clothes, fruits and some money all arranged in a silver plate, from the party concerned. After the function is solemnized, they all bless him and pray for his longevity. According to the practice followed by the Maithil Brahmins of this State, the girl is shown to the members of the boy's family immediately after the Wakya Dan.

As the boy's parents, prior to the finalisation of marriage proposal, obtain informations secretly through their kins about the nature and beauty of the girl, there is perhaps hardly any possibility left for the rejection of the girl when shown to them after the Wakya Dan.

The fact that the girl is not shown to the members of the boy's family at any stage of marriage among the Yadavas, indicates that they despise the practice of observing Cheka for the bride as prevalent among the Maithil Brahmins and the inferior castes in the village and elsewhere in the state. Like the Brahmins, the Yadavas also do not go to the parents of the girl, as is done by the lower and untouchable castes, for the marriage of their sons. Hence, it is the girl's parents who approach the boy's parents for their daughter's marriage and observe the Cheka ceremony of the boy but without any reciprocity.

Betrothal (Tilak) ceremony is the second stage, and lastly, marriage is performed. On an auspicious day members of the girl's family come to pay the dowry that includes, besides clothes and utensils, the sum promised. The practice is too much in vogue among the the upper castes except the Maithils in the State. In the village the amount of dowry, among the Yadavas, varies from Rs. 500/- to Rs 10,000/-. Recently the well-to-do families of the lower castes have also adopted this practice.

At last, marriage takes place. A party of relations, friends and other invitees proceed with the groom to the bride's place where all necessary arrangements for their reception and stay are made on behalf of the girl's family. After a few hours in the night, the groom is taken in a procession on a horseback or in a car (previously in a palanquin), according to one's status, to his father-in-law's house where marriage is performed at the appropriate time. The bride and her parents or any other couple superior in age and status, who perform the rites of giving her in marriage, must take their ritual bath and observe fast on that day. The bridegroom also takes proper bath, changes his sacred thread if it is the marriage of a

Brahmin boy, observes fast and puts on new clothes. Among the Yadavas, the sacred thread ceremony (Upanayan) is performed at the time of marriage. All rites relating to marriage are performed by the priest according to Vedic style.

After staying for nearly two days, members of the marriage party (Barati), accompanied by the bride and the bridegroom, take leave of their hosts. Besides money, clothes, and utensils, which were received by the boy's parents at the time of betrothal, a few articles of daily use including cots, beds, cycle, wrist watch, pen, radio, money and clothes according to the status of the father-in-law, are also given to the bridegroom in marriage. The bride's departure presents a heart-breaking scene as she weeps joined by other women of the house and of the locality for leaving parents and joining the family of her husband.

Rituals of Death

Death occurring on Tuesday or Saturday is believed to be inauspicious by the people of all castes in the village. To ward off the supposed danger to any one in the family consequent upon such death, a black pigeon and a little mustard of yellowish colour wrapped in a piece of black cloth are burnt together with the dead body. None except the family members of the deceased have the right to perform rites connected with death. Moreover, among the Brahmins and the Yadavas, it is the members of the family who, first of all, carry the bier from the house to some distance when others join them in the procession.

After a proper bath, the deceased is kept on the pyre at the bank of the sacred Ganges with the head lying northward and the legs stretched southward. Generally, the eldest son performs the fire-giving ceremony. A small piece of sandal wood, with one of its two ends wrapped in cloth and having a little quantity of ghee sprinkled over it, is kept burning with which the pyre is lit. But before doing so, one has to go thrice round the pyre, holding the other end of the sandal wood in the left hand and each time getting the navel feet and lastly the mouth touched with it amidst of Vedic mantras. The corpse is burnt into ashes; however, at least one tenth of its charred portion is retained, which is thrown into the river for the animals living in it. The tradition of immersing ashes into sacred rivers at various holy places in the country is unknown to the people. Hence, the place is fully washed out and the processionists, after writing five times the name of Lord Ram, move towards another bank of the river for a purificatory bath. The nearest kins offer water with their left hand to the departed soul. Among the lower castes, the Karta, who performs the fire-giving ceremony, gets his head and beard shaved.

On the third day the Karta offers oblation (Pinda) thrice to the departed soul at a fixed place usually close to a river or a pond. Male members of the family also join him in offering thrice a little mustard oil and its chaff, whereas females only take regular but full purificatory bath. On the seventh day seven oblations and on the tenth day ten oblations for equal number of times are offered to the dead.

On the tenth day, the period of pollution ends with the shaving of head and beard (Chour Karma). The Yadavas and the Brahmins observe it on the tenth day, whereas all other castes, including the untouchables, do it on the completion of a month. However, due to Sanskritization, observance of Chour Karma by the untouchables on the completion of a month is fast disappearing. For nine days the beard is allowed to grow and on the tenth day, when the period of impurity is over, the head and beard are shaved. It is not only the members of the family but also the near kins who get their head and beard shaved and replace their old earthen vessels by new ones.

If any bereavement occurs in a poor family of a Choudhary, it causes much financial strain on the members because Choudharies living in the village and in the adjoining areas have close kinship relationship and, therefore, they all are invited to the feasts for three days. For the purpose of interdining on ceremonial occasions, the Choudharies maintain two divisions called

Chati among themselves. One Chati includes members of families from five to seven generations. Families in one Chati need not invite families in the other to the ceremonial feasts which relieves the host of inviting quite a large number of people. As families in both the groups have close kinship relationship they equally observe the period of mourning and of pollution. The ceremony comes to an end with the Sapinda Karma usually observed on the eleventh and twelfth day, after which the soul is believed to have joined the family of dead ancestors. Oblation are offered to the deceased and to a number of dead ancestors. A variety of things like, clothes, utensils, beds and cots which the deceased was fond of are given to the priest on the supposition that these things would gratify him even after death. In the death of a young man, the intensity of suffering and mourning are naturally great and the Karta observes fast for almost ten days. Besides a large number of Brahmins, relatives and friends who attend the cremation are fed on the twelfth day.

A few among the rich persons belonging to the upper castes at Bharko also go to Gaya to offer oblations to their dead ancestors. After it is finished, they take a sigh of relief and return home with a feeling that they have paid their debt to their dead ancestors. About Gaya Shraddha, Professor L. P. Vidhyarthi (1961:31:34) writers :

> "The most important single sacred performance at Gaya is the Shraddha Yajna (ancestor sacrifice) which is performed every year by more than 80,000 Hindus coming from different parts of India. Shraddha at Gaya is essentially observed in honour of the dead fathers and other progenitors and should be distinguished from the rites which immediately follow death (Mrityu Sanskar or death sacrament), subsequent anniversary ancestor worship (Varshik Shraddha) or the annual ritual calendric ancestor worship (Mahalaya or Jitiya). While there are several common elements among the four forms of ancestor worship, the very fact that Gaya Shraddha is observed at a public sacred ground rather than a domestic and local sacred centre and that its success brings final emancipation to the ancestors and happiness to

the survivors gives its performance all possible elaboration seriousness and sacredness".[10]

Festivals

The ritual aspect of Hinduism consists mainly of festivals, fasts, feasts, charity, pilgrimage, etc. which for the most part, constitute village religion. R.B. Chauhan (1967:182) outlines the meaning of ritual structure thus :

"The ritual structure of a society defines those aspects in the life of the people which they can associate with the supernatural and about which they have been able to find some ways of negotiation".[11]

This is exactly what happens in a developed and complex society. But what is much more significant from the point of view of a village community is the useful or practical nature of religion. Religion and rituals have already been discussed. Now it becomes imperative to discuss the festival cycle so that the ritual structure of the village is presented in its full form.

Study of festivals broadly helps to uncover the patterns of religious behaviour of the people of various groups in a society. Besides, research into festivals focuses light on several other issues; for example, the general role of festivals in the social life of the people, the degree of integration between the 'great' and 'little' tradition of Hinduism, the amount of caste and community participation, the amount of increase or decrease in caste distinctions, the degree of what Marriott calls 'Universalization' and 'Parochialization' or what Srinivas calls national, regional and local spread, the association of festivals with agricultural activities and lastly, the patterns of change. Marriott (1955:193) observes :

"The great tradition of Hinduism is not merely present as a part of most festivals of Kishan Garhi, but it has achieved, through the festivals, an integrated position in village life. Great festivals of Sanskritic rationale and nomenclature provide, along with domestic ceremonies, the principal occasions on which most villagers may engage in concerted symbolic activities."[12]

Recent investigations into village festivals have thrown sufficient light on the above aspects of the subject. Lewis, Marriott, Dube and Srinivas have attempted to present a classification of festivals and ceremonies into working types but without any lasting success as the task has really proved very difficult. Dr. Dube (1955:96) classifies ceremonies and village ceremonies.[13] But the same may be applicable to Shamirpet only and may not easily be distinguished in other villages. The basic problem is to suggest sound scientific classifications and types so that all festivals, rituals and ceremonies can easily be distinguised, separated and even integrated on the basis of common properties or ingredients for all times to come. Professor Lewis (1958:197:198) summarises the difficulty involved in such a work and puts his note of warning against a hasty classification of festivals thus :

> "Any analysis of Indian festivals, whether it be historical or functional, should be based upon descriptions of the ceremonial cycle followed in a variety of specific communities. Until we have such data, it will not be possible to assess the role of the Hindu festivals in Indian life and the varying degrees of integration in different localities between the 'great' and 'little' traditions of Hinduism".[14]

Marriott warns those who are promptly to identify all village festivals with the great Sanskritic tradititionn. For evaluating the issue of identification, Marriot (1955:193:194:195) compares the festivals in Kishan Garhi with the great Sanskritic tradition in the following four ways :

(i) those festivals which have no evident Sanskritic rationales;

(ii) those festivals which do have Sanskritic rationales represent only a small selection;

(iii) between the festivals of Kishan Garhi and those sanctioned by the great tradition, connections are often loosened, confused, or mistaken because of a multiplicity of combeting meanings for each special day within the great tradition itself ; and

(iv) behind their Sanskritic names and multiple great traditional rationales, the festivals of Kishan Garhi contain much ritual which has no evident connection wiih the great tradition.[15]

First it is proposed to begin with a list of important festivals at Bharko and then to report the degree of their identification with the great Sanskritic tradition, keeping however, in mind Marriott's note of warning.

The following illustrate the festival cycle as observed at Bharko :—

Ramnavmi, Bisua, Ghato and Dora—Chaitra (March-April); Barsaeet—Jyestha (May-June); Shravani Amabashya and Rakhi—Shrawan (July-August); Krishnasthami, Teej, Chakchanda, Karmadharma, Vishwakarma Puja and Anant-Bhadra (August-September); Pitri Parba, Jitia and Durga Puja—Ashwin (September-October); Deepawali, Chhatt, Gopasthami, Devothan Ekadasi and Kartika Purnima—Kartika (October-November); Nawann-Agrahan (November-December); Tilasankranti—Pausha (December-January), Basant Panchmi and Maghi Purnima—Maghra (January-February) and lastly, Shivaratri and Holi—Phalgun (February-March).

Ramnavmi

This festival is a survival of the great tradition of Hinduism and, as such, is celebrated in all thc four corners of the country. It falls on the ninth-day of the bright fortnight of Chaitra and is observed as the birthday of Lord Ram. It is expected that members of the whole community, irrespective of their caste or economic positions, would observe the day with devotion and purity, but in practice it is not found to be so. In the village only the four castes—Brahmin, Yadavas, Baniya and Surhi observe it, though it is obligatory for all the Hindus of the village to do so. Mahabir Asthan, Bhagwati Asthan and Thakurbari are whitewashed and their doors decorated with flowers, festoons and banana plants and leaves.

The floor and courtyard of residential houses are cleansed with dung mixed in water. Proper bath is a prerequisite to all kinds of ceremonial worships. On the previous day, before taking either breakfast or meal (Nahakha), the devotees are required to bath properly. On the following day men and women, after taking bath, observe fast till midday and break it by taking first five ingredients (Panchamrit) and food (Prasad) offered to the deity. Afterwards, they all take their usual food. A few among the ardent devotees, mostly widows, prefer to observe fast for the whole day and night.

The Brahmins celebrate it in their own houses; the Baniyas and the Surhis in the Mahabir Asthan and the Yadavas in the Thakurbari. In the Thakurbari images of Ram, Sita, Laxman and Hanuman are kept on a wooden stool in the centre of the place of worship. Young boys show much enthusiasm in organizing a cultural function in the night for which funds are collected in advance. The day is marked by prayers and devotional songs and the night by dramas staged by the local youngsters. Besides, several Sankritan Mandalis consisting of groups of people including the devotees move in a procession with banners and musical instruments singing and dancing from one local shrine to the other around the village.

The highlight of the festival is the ceremonial installation of Hanuman flag (Dwaja) in the courtyards of residential houses. The belief surrounding such installation is that the presence of Hanuman in the house is enough to thwart any attempt by ghosts or spirits to harm the inmates.

Bisua

The festival falls on the fourth day of the bright fornight of Chaitra. It is known as Bisua only in this region, though in other parts of the State it is known as Satuani. Its Sanskritized name is Chaitra Sankranti. Sankranti is connected with the movement of the sun from its one position to another. The festival essentially relates to the worship of the sun and is unfailingly observed, after the harvest of Rabi crops, by all agriculturists of the village. The festival is particularly marked by taking after proper bath and observance of fast till midday, gram and barley powder (Sattu) by the people. Brahmins are fed Sattu on this day as it is considered virtuous.

Ghato

This festival is also observed by women of all castes except the exterior untouchable castes in the village. It relates to the worship of the sun and continues for six months, i.e., from Agrahan to Vaishakh. Women occupy positions almost in a circlie around a Pipal tree to the trunk of which they tie a coloured thread (Dora). They also tie five silken threads to their left hand above the elbow. They all rise early in the morning and, after taking bath, assemble near the tree for worship. They offer thread, betel, betel-nut and some sweets to the sun every day in the morning and they promise in worship to offer the Sun-God Dora as usual if the economic conditions of their families improve. Besides, telling stories among themselves at the place of worship is the characteristic feature of the festival. It is only after they have finished their stories concerning sun-worship that they disperse.

Barsaeet

It falls on the last day of the first fortnight of Jyestha. Like the previous two festivals, it is also confined to the women folk except that only married women belonging to the Kulin castes celebrate it. In the village it is celebrated mostly by the Brahmin women, though recently women in the Choudhary families have also started celebrating it. The sole purpose underlying the celebration of this festival is to offer prayer for the longevity of the husband or for freedom from widowhood and barrenness. Its Sanskritized name is Batshavitri and is very popular among women of Kulin castes in different parts of the country. Its brief story is as follows :

> Savitri, the daughter of a king was married to Satyawan who was also the son of a king. It was prophesied that Satyawan would remain alive only for a year after his

marriage. Despite the prophesy, Savitri married Satyawan because she had already accepted him within her heart to be her husband. After marriage she began to maintain the righteousness of chastity and dutiful devotion towards her husband, but on the final day when both went to a forest a venomous snake bit Satyawan who died immediately.

The demon-king (Yamraj) who takes away the soul after death appeared as usual but did not do so as he was much impressed by her prayer and indelible chastity.

Since then Savitri is worshipped as an idol of chastity and consecration. For Indian women, particulary of Kulin castes, widowhood is regarded as the highest curse of God and barrenness as the greatest misfortune.

Women observe fast for the whole day and night. During day time, after proper bath, they go to the outskirts of the village for the worship of a tree called Bat. They sit in a circle round the tree and offer flowers, vermillion, rice, sweets and pieces of red and yellow cloth. Thrice they go round the tree and every time they tie a long red thread to the trunk of the tree. The priest recites the story (Katha) of Sati Savitri which they hear with rapt attention. When this is over, a moment is spent in meditation and then they all disperse.

Shravani Amabashya

This festival falls on the last day of the first fortnight of Shravan; and is particularly observed by the newly wedded girls belonging to the Maithil Brahmin caste all over Bihar. On this occasion it is customary for the father to send clothes and sweets to his daughter if she is at her father-in-law's place (Sasural), but if she is at her father's place, it is the father-in-law who sends these things to her.

After proper bath, these newly married girls put on new clothes sent by their fathers or father-in-laws, as the case may be, and then go to the local shrines for worship. All of them observe complete fast on this day; and, besides flowers, fruits, vermillion, clothes and sweets, prayers are offered to the deities for a long and happy conjugal life. Again after proper both and a little worship (Puja), they break their fast on the next day.

Rakhi

This is an important festival falling on the last day of the month of Shravan. Rakhi is a multicoloured thread and is tied to the wrist of a person and is known as Raksha Bandhan. Its importance for the people is very great because the thread is believed to be a symbol of safety (Raksha) against any catastrophe in future. When the people are free from their morning bath, the priests, one after another, come to tie the thread, for which the latter are paid either in cash or kind. Nobody returns from the priest, in whatever number they may come, without paying something for fear of being born as a destitute in his or her next life. More or less the entire village observes it and in that way it benefits the Brahmins. Though it is unknown in villages, however, in towns and cities, sisters in rich families bind the thread in the hands of their brothers and receive money or gifts in return from them. Those who are living with their husbands and are, therefore, unable to come, send the thread by post. The day is marked by special dishes served by the female to the male members of the family.

Besides, the month is considered significant for two more celebrations, namely, Sombari and Jhulan. During Sombari, both men and women take morning bath and go to the Shiva temple for worship. They pour Ganges water over the image of Lord Shiva, offer him Bel leaves and flowers, and lastly, pray for the betterment of their economic condition. Women observe fast on all the four or five Mondays (Sombar) falling in the month. Except the untouchable castes, all other castes offer prayer and worship to the deity but the most prominent among these are the Brahmin, Yadava and Surhi. A few persons go to Baidyanath Dham, Deoghar, which is about forty miles away from the village, for the worship of Lord Shiva over there. Those who cannot afford to undertake the journey visit Jethaurnath temple situated at eight miles from the village and the rest worship the deity in the local shrine. At Deoghar a large number of pilgrims, both from the state and outside, can be seen on these days. In the village, people visit the local Shivalaya again in the evening to have a view of the decorated deity or either join other devotees in singing devotional songs or leave after a little prayer or worship.

Jhulan is celebrated in the Thakurbari for about three days in the last week of the month. The celebrations end on the Rakhi day. Images of Lord Krishna and Radha, are kept on a small swinging seat which the priest sways at frequent intervals with the help of a silken thread tied to the seat. As the place of celebration is kept open from evening to midnight large number of men, women and children come to the Thakurbari to have a view of the deities and receive Prasad. The Yadavas organize either musical programme or Bhajan (singing of devotional songs) in the Thakurbari on all the three days.

Krishnasthami

On the eighth day of Bhadra (August-September), the Hindus all over India celebrate Krishnasthami—the birthday of Lord Krishna. The Yadavas, much less the Baniyas and the Surhis in the village, celebrate it with great enthusiasm and piety. On the day, the people assemble in the Thakurbari and leave it only when given Prasad by the temple priest who ends the worship of the Lord with burning candles (Arati) kept in a dish in which people put some coins out of reverence. Most of the people, who keep fast, break it in the noon-time by taking fruits (Phalahar). Only a few continue it for the whole day and night.

Teej

The festival dates back to the mythical Parvati undergoing penance in order to have Shiva as her husband. Women-folk, mostly of the Brahmin and Yadava castes of the village, celebrate the Teej festival on the third day of the bright fort-night of Bhadra and worship Parvati to get her blessings for a long and happy conjugal life as well as to have the same husbands in the next birth. On the day, women observe a total fast and refuse to drink even a single drop of water, they dare not break it for fear of divine curse. With great enthusiam they prepare varieties of food to be offered to the deity at the time of worshlp which is done in a group consisting of four or five women listening with a reverential awe the story (Katha) being narrated. With its end the first day of their penance is over but they break their fast only on the second day early in the morning. On this occasion women decorate themselves with their ornaments and newly married girls get a gift of new clothes from their father-in-laws.

Chakchanda

On the next day of Teej falls the festival named Chakchanda celebrated equally by women of low castes and by school-going children of the village. Women are, however, ignorant of its basic significance as a day of worship of Lord Ganesh; they simply observe fast wishing the welfare of their children. But children worship Lord Ganesh in their schools, sing songs and play with two small wooden sticks (Gulli Danda). Seeing the moon on this night is supposed to be inauspicious.

Karmadharma

It is an Ekadashi (eleventh day of the month) observed chiefly by women of the lower castes and by unmarried girls of the Brahmin and Yadava castes as a day of worship of the sun. However, they have distinct ways of observing it. Married women of the lower castes observe it by digging a small trench and making images of mud in it; all this is done for the welfare of their husbands and children. Whereas the unmarried girls of the Brahmin and Yadav castes jump across the trench with the help of their younger brothers, the women of the lower castes put a thorny plant in it and worship it by keeping fast for the whole day.

Vishwakarma Puja

The artisans — carpenters, blacksmiths, goldsmiths etc.— celebrate this festival with great pomp and worship

Vishwakarma, the great divine designer. For them it is the day of joy and feast.

Anant

Except the untouchables all other castes, particularly the Yadavas and the Brahmins, celebrate this festival by gathering at different places, listening to the tale (Katha) being narrated by a Brahmin-priest who ends it by worshipping a number of sacred threads (Anant) which are then distributed among their owners. Men wear the anant on the right arm and women on the left arm. The celebration concludes with a family-feast.

Pitri-Parva

The Brahmins, the Yadavas, the Baniyas and the Surhis of the village celebrate this festival for fifteen days in the first fortnight of Ashwin by worshipping their dead ancestors and offering them water, rice, and Til; all this is done under the direction of a Brahmin priest. Except a few well-to-do Yadavas and Surhis who manage to go to Gaya for performing this rite, most of the people do it in the village itself. For fifteen days people lead an austere life. On the fifteenth day they get their hairs shaved, take purificatory bath, offer oblations to the dead souls and feed the Brahmins sumptuously.

Jitia

Women, even old mothers having sufficiently grown-up children, celebrate this festival by keeping fast for a day and worshipping different local and famiiy deities for the protection of their children against future calamity. They distribute their Prasad among their children and thus bless them. The fast is broken the next morning.

Durga Puja

On the tenth day of the bright fortnight of Ashwin, all and sundry celebrate this most important festival of the Hindus by worshipping the image of Mother Durga or Bhagwati as an incarnation of invincible power, a killer of demons and Satans and a bestower of divine grace for success in life. On this day people also celebrate the victory of the mythical Ram over the demon King—Ravana. Ten days of celebration are maked by gaiety, rejoicings and chiefly by animal sacrifice made to the Goddess on two days, i.e., on the eighth and ninth days of worship. At the Bhagwati Asthan (temple) sacrifices of goats are made in a serial number in order to avoid unnecessary conflict. Sacrifices are also made in the homes of the Brahmins. The total number of sacrifices in the village comes to 150 every year. The whole village assumes a festive look with men, women and children clad in new clothes and moving from one place to another. The whole village hums with a new life. Forgetting their divisions and feuds people take part in cultural entertainments and in decorating the image of the Goddess as well as the temple. All this comes to an end on the tenth day when the image is taken in a procession and, at last, immersed in a nearby rivulet.

Deepawali

With great enthusiasm and expectation people wait for the first fortnight of Kartika when they celebrate the Deepawali—the festival of burning lights and praying to God for the divine light—'Tamso ma Jyotirgamaya' (lead, kindly light, from darkness to light) symbolised by the burning of small earthen lamps on the streets and over the houses. Throughout there is only light and no trace of darkness for the whole of night. People celebrate it with the faith that Goddess Lakshmi (Goddess of Wealth) visits the houses on the enlightened night. Thus the villagers keep their houses perfectly neat and clean and in good order. Baniyas, Surhis and the businessmen in general worship the Goddess Lakshmi on that night with a hope of gaining profit in business.

Chhatt

Of all the Hindu festivals this is the most dreadful. Women of all castes worship the rising and the setting Sun-God by undergoing penance and fast and by offering fruits, water and milk to him by the side of the Ganges or a river or a pond.

Perfect purity of the worshipper and of the things offered to the sun must be maintained, otherwise the worshipper might be cursed with white leprosy. The third day, which is the last day of worship, is the most difficult day for the female-devotees have to stand deep in the cold water of the Ganges or the river or the pond and offer prayers to the Sun-God. For the first two days the worshippers have to take only the prescribed meal consisting of Araba rice (unboiled rice), pulse etc. It is celebrated for the welfare of husbands, children and other members of the family.

Gopasthami

It is a festival of cow-worship celebrated by the Yadavas and the Brahmins of the village. They put new strings decorated with dangling bells round the necks of their cows and offer them grass and sweet-meats.

Devothan Ekadasi

People celebrate this festival in order to worsnip Lord Vishnu—Lord, and sustainer, by putting His image on a wooden plank surrounded by standing sugarcanes. The Yadavas celebrate it in the Thakurbari, the Brahmins in their houses, the Surhis and the Baniyas in the Shivalaya.

Kartika Purnima

On the last day of the month of Kartika people of all rank and file take a holy dip in the Ganges. For that they go even to distant places.

Nawann

In the month of Agrahan, when the first harvest of paddy crop is over, the festival of Nawann is celebrated by agriculturists throughout the rural region of Bhagalpur, which is one of the prominent rice-producing centres in the State of Bihar. This festival is peculiar only to this region.

Tila Sankranti

This festival falls in the winter season and is observed by all the Hindus in the village. It is significant for giving Til

(Sesame) in charity to the Brahmins who are also fed chipped rice and curd. Houses are kept neat and clean and their floors washed with cow-dung. After usual bath in the morning, people offer Til to the Sun-God and worship it. The food which is eaten on this day consists mainly of Til, chipped rice and curd. Besides the Brahmins, friends and relativas are also fed on this day.

Basant Panchmi

On the fifth day of the bright fortnight of Magh people celebrate Basant Panchmi—the spring festival in various forms. The villagers keep fast on this day and go to worship Lord Shiva of the famous Ajgaibinath temple situated at the top of a hill some eight miles away from Bharko. Yadava and Brahmin women worship the family God and keep fast on that day. In the evening jubilant people assemble at local shrines to sing songs and besmear one another with coloured powder.

Student celebrate it by installing the image of Goddess Saraswati (Goddess of Learning) in their respective institutions. The occasion is marked by great festivity and cultural shows.

Maghi Purnima

On the last day of the month of Magh people take bath in the holy Ganges, go to the temple to worship various gods and then eat on the banks of the Ganges. On this occasion also people go to the Ajgaibinath temple to worship Lord Shiva.

Shivaratri

The fourth day of the dark fortnight of Phalgun brings Shivaratri—a festival when men and women worship Lord Shiva to get the divine blessings. People worship the Lord in Shivalayas with all obeisance and pomp. Females outnumber males in observing fast on the day. Women, married or unmarried, are seen visiting the temple twice—once in the morning and then again in the evening. In the night devotees assemble in a large number in the Shivalaya to observe the decorated

Lord Shiva being worshipped by the priest and to take part in the singing of devotional songs.

Holi

Holi—a festival of joy and merriment, of unity and cordiality, of intercaste and inter-family relations—is celebrated by men and women, young and old alike. On this occasion people greet even their enemies. Besides, the feeling of oneness pervades those members of a consanguine family who are now living separately as well as those of the joint family. The occasion is marked by the slinging of mud, dust and coloured water. On this occasion people celebrate the death of the mythical lady named HOLIKA, the sister of king Hirankashyapu who wanted his son Prahalad to die for uttering the name of Lord Narayan and not accepting him, i.e., the King as the Almighty Lord. To lesson her brother's anxiety HOLIKA, with the little Prahalad in her lap, put herself in the midst of the burning fire with a hope that whereas he will be burnt to death, she will come out alive since she had the divine blessing that fire could never burn her. But her hope was soon shattered, she was burnt to death and Prahalad came out unburnt. To celebrate it, people burn faggots. People wear new clothes and eat delicious food. In the evening people in groups move and besmear coloured powder on faces. It is a festival when people are free to eat, drink and be merry.

REFERENCES

CHAPTER VII

1. Mathur, K.S., 1964, *Caste and Ritual in a Malwa Village,* (Asia Publishing House, Bombay).

2. Srinivas, M.N., 1952, *Religion And Society Among the Coorgs of South India,* (Oxford University Press. Amen House, London, E.C. 4).

3. Dube, S.C., 1955, *Indian Village,* (Routledge & Kegan Paul Ltd; London, E.C. 4).

4. Opler, Morris E., 1950, *Village Life in North India*'—Quoted by Oscar Lewis in *Village Life in Northern India;* (University of Illinois Press, Urbana, U.S.A.), 1958, P. 251.

5. Radhakrishnan, S., 1961, *The Hindu View of Life,* (George Allen & Unwin Ltd; London, W.C. 1).

6. *Ibid.*

7. Singh, T.R., 1966, '*Some Aspects of Ritual Purity And Pollution*'—Eastern Anthropologist, Vol. XIX, No. 2, May-August, The Ethnographic & Folk-Culture Society (U.P.), Lucknow (India).

8. Sharma, K.N., 1961, *Hindu Sects And Food Patterns In North India*, P. 2.

Aspects of Religion in Indian Society, Ed. by L.P. Vidyarthi, Kedar Nath Ram Nath, Meerut City.

9. *Ibid.*

10. Chauhan, B.R., 1967, *A Rajasthan Village,* (Vir Publishing House, New Delhi-5).

11. Vidyarthi, L.P., 1961, *Sacred Complex In Hindu Gaya,* Asia Publishing House, Bombay).

12. Marriot, Mackim, 1955, "*The Little Communities In An Indigenous Civilization*", *Village,* ed, by Mckim, Marriott, (University of Chicago Press, Chicago, U.S.A).

13. *Ibid.*

14. Lewis, Oscar, 1958, *Village Life In Northern India,* (University of Illinois Press, Urbana, U.S.A).

CHAPTER VIII

Conclusion

Bharko, like many other Indian villages, is very much sensitive to the present-day social and economic changes. To proclaim, as the Westerners do, that Indian villages are insusceptible to any appreciable change, is to misjudge the things. Despite the alleged indifference of the Britishers to rural upliftment in India, the rural communities witnessed imperceptible changes in their institutions and organizations. Quite apart from the research works of several sociologists and anthropologists, the microcosmic or microsociological study of even a randomly selected village like Bharko reveals this fact about changes in the Indian countryside, particularly after the liquidation of the British rule. Some of the most striking changes that have occurred in the village are to be enumerated in this Chapter, although it is very difficult to account for all of them.

In the first place, mention must be made of the changes in what Professor Srinivas (1959:2) calls the 'decisive dominance' of the Yadavas and the consequential modifications in the social structure or the interrelations between the twentytwo castes in the village. The concept of dominant caste itself undergoes a change and is reservedly applied after the establishment of a statutory village panchayat and the introduction of new patterns of land relations consequent upon the abolition of the Zamindari system. No doubt, the Yadavas are numerically, economically and politically the strongest of all, but this does not mean that a few other castes like the Brahmin and the Surhi, which are economically quite well off, have no influence in the affairs of the village. Except the Choudharies and a few Mahtos, the rest among the Yadavas are poor and needy. Recent improvement in the socio-economic status of the Brahmins and the Surhis has weakened the age old decisive dominance of the Yadavas, the village is said to be dominated today by the Brahmins and the Surhis as well. This has led to new alignments in the interpersonal relationships between the owner and the tenant, the patron and the client, members of one caste and those of another. The interrelations of various groups and classes now bear quite a different look from what it was in the past and the village may be said to have undergone remarkable structural changes.

Further, the emergence of these two powerful castes in the village has its repercussion on the traditional structure of authority and power hitherto absolutely exercised by the Yadavas; and this fact has eventually led to the formation of new faction groups or parties, i.e., a new form of social dynamics in the viliage. The village is internally too much faction-ridden and its old corpoarate unity is now marked by mounting jealousy, tension and conflict prevailing among the three castes namely the Yadavas, the Brahmins and the Surhis. More than the Surhis, whom both the Brahmins and the Yadavas despise for their lower caste status, the Brahmins are hostile and inimical to the Yadavas, though they outwardly maintain family and friendly relations with them. On many occasions both the Brahmins and Yadavas have fought and taken recourse to legal actions to settle their disputes.

As for the development of the village, the Brahmins invariably withhold their cooperation to the Yadavas and even indirectly endeavour to spoil their initiative, with the result that the progress of the village is retarded. A few instances which prove the non-cooperation of the Brahmins are—setting up a village high school by the Yadavas, purchase of the weekly market from the Government, settlement of disputes and even the execution of the development schemes of the village panchayat or of the Block. The Brahmins, who are at the top tier of caste hierarchy, have considerably improved their socio-economic status and, therefore, they no longer want to remain under the authority and leadership of the Yadavas who are much inferior to them in caste position. Besides jealousy and pride in equal economic status, the super-ordination and subordination of caste may be a reason for the hostile attitude on the part of the Brahmins. Because in the past when the economic condition of the Brahmins was deplorable, they used to receive threats and insults from the Yadavas, the status to which the Brahmins of Kumbapettai have been reduced today. Kathleen Gough (1955:46) describes this situation in these words: 'In other ways, the breakdown of the feudal economic system, the emergence of lower-caste groups in economic rivalry rather than cooperation, and the widening range of social relations beyond the village have endangered the power of the Brahmins and the unity of Kumbapettai.' Rivalry and conflict between the Brahmins and the Yadavas become apparent every time during elections to the office of the Mukhiya and the Surpanch for the village panchayat. The Brahmins are much more polished and intricate in action and behaviour than their enemies.

The change in the structure of authority and power is significantly a modern feature of the village. The traditional authority of caste panchayat and of village leaders has today immensely weakened as is evident from infrequent commissions of serious caste and other acts of violation. Certain castes have caste panchayats but these do not justify their existence except that they mostly perform the political functions. On the contrary, the statutory village panchayat wields authority and power for the entire village and promises to bring about rapid progress in the socio-economic and cultural life of the farmers in the countryside. The new panchayat, the highest elected body armed with both the executive and the judiciary power, is a wonderful experiment in village reconstruction and development. It aims at establishing the panchayati Raj in the country based on democratic decentralization of power. This change in the structure of authority and power has given a new life and awakening to the villagers with the result that a new pattern of village organization has begun to emerge. If the village panchayat works on a sound footing by undertaking to fulfil most of its defined functions, the face of Indian villages is bound to change.

The influence of city life, apart from other things, on the pattern of social relationships among members of the community appears to be great. Earlier it has been mentioned that the village is linked with Bhagalpur, a business or commercial town, throught regular bus services. Quite a large number of pepole of this villages as well as of the adjoining villages go to Bhagalpur for many works. A sizeable number of landless or otherwise economically oppressed people are absorbed in different jobs over there. Frequent contacts with towns and cities thus widen social relations and influence the ideological, cultural and behaviour patterns of the villagers. Outside contact has also led to the development of individualistic, selfish and separatist tendencies among them. The glamour of village life in respect of cooperative unity, functional interdependence of various castes and unsophisticated nature of social and personal relationships is fast decaying. Groups and factions that are constantly engaged in engineering caste and political rivalry, hostility and mutual distrust and which pattern feelings and behaviour of the people make the village life appear distinct from what it was in the past. The growing discontentment, quite a recent development among the villagers, makes social life difficult to live and requires a new adjustment on the part of the members. The appalling situations responsible for increasing complexity and intricacy in the social and personal life of the people were revealed during an open interview with them. Such changes in social relations are accompanied by significant structural variations which the Indian villages are witnessing today.

Urban influence, as usual, proves advantageous to the farmers in many important spheres of their life. Besides bringing about changes in thoughts and habits, living and working conditions, culture and personality, the tangible results of urban influence are—the middle and the high schools, improved agricultural practices, the metalled road linking the village with the world outside, cooperative societies, trade and business, medical facilities, mill or factory made goods and commodities and replacement of old norms and values by new ones.

Another feature of change noticeable in the village is the mobility in caste hierarchy and occupation. The tables presented by Professor Srinivas (1966:97:99) do not require further facts about caste mobility in the country. No doubt caste exists as a rigid social institution regulating and determining social relations and cultural patterns of its members. It is hereditary and as such fixes one's position in the society and transmits culture and skills. Not only does it reflect the horizontal strata into which the whole village society is stratified but it also defines the area of marriage along with certain taboos and religious duties for each of them.

Notwithstanding the aforesaid functions and obligations, the institution of caste undergoes a process of gradual transformation in the village.

Except the endogamous and ritual character which it retains steadily and continuously it has shirked most of its other duties and responsibilities. In view of the dissolution of its cultural functions along with certain institutional ones like taboos or restrictions on interdining and observance of untouchability people in the village have begun to feel that the barriers of caste have perhaps broken away. Pointing out the disintegration of caste E.R. Leach (1960:6) questions, "If a caste group turns into a political faction does it then cease to be a caste ? This is exactly what happens in Indian village today. Villagers seldom conform to the outward expressions or manifestations of caste except that caste is held as a form of social identity."

The contention of D. Sivertsen (1963:10) that caste conflicts as related to the economic order and to existing political arrangements have disrupted today the hierarchical order within caste is noteworthy.

There are multiple factors, namely, modernization, industrialization, urbanization, democracy, education etc. which have struck at the very root of the caste system. Love and inter-caste marriage have made their passage deep into the village. Earlier in the chapter on caste structure two cases of inter-caste marriage from the village have already been referred. Defiance of caste principle by the people has thus become very frequent.

Again, caste is reinforced by religious sanctions and practices and fixes one's place in the socio-religous life of the community. However, these sanctions and practices seem to have dwindled before people's love for wealth and other economic gains. Villagers have started paying little attention to the traditionally defined or demarcated positions—superior and inferior, of various castes. In the internal organization and administration of the village, the Yadavas occupy the highest position but what is more ostensible is the wholesale disrespect to or the wilful ignorance of the position of the Brahmins by the former. Of course, the situation has greatly changed as the Brahmins have considerably raised their socio-economic position and are treated now as equal to the Choudharies. Likewise, the Surhis, who belong to the category of the unclean caste, enjoy a high and prestigious position even in the eyes of the Brahmins and the Yadavas for the simple reason that they are the wealthy traders in the village. On the contrary, a few other castes which are much more superior to the Surhis in caste position are not considered so both by the Brahmins and the Yadavas for the fact that they are poor and landless. Although it appears as irrelevant but the fact is that the Brahmins have aligned with the Surhis for political purposes. From this it is safely inferred that an increase in the economic and political status of a caste, even though it may have a lower caste status, helps it to climb the hierarchical order. A few cases of families which have changed their caste are already known to us.

Further, occupational mobility is no longer a distant dream of the people belonging to various castes in the village. A few cases of a change in caste occupation are being mentioned here. A Brahmin whose income from the traditional caste occupation has been meagre runs a fair price shop and deals in medicine. The richest man of his caste is a government contractor. A few Yadavas have entered the business field. The Chamars and the Julahas work as ploughmen for the Yadavas and the Brahmins. A barber is working as the Gramsewak, a paid servant of the government, in the Office of the Village Panchayat. Castes and families depending on the Jajmani system have taken to new occupations as a result of which the system has begun to disappear. Likewise, forces and factors responsible for the observance of untouchability have totally disintegrated bringing the social distance to a minimum in the village.

Lastly, the process of Sanskritization at work among the lower castes causes the petrifying and stationary nature of caste to change. The significant development in this direction has not only been the adoption of the customs and manners of the titles and surnames of the upper castes by the lower ones. The following castes have changed their caste names and titles :

Surhi to Saundik Vaishya,
Beldar to Bindh,
Julaha as Tantu Vaishya,
Chamar to Harijan,
Dhobi to Rajak; and, again,
Kamar to Sharma,
Nai to Thakur,
Kahar to Singh etc.

In this connection A. Aiyappan's observation (1965:174:176) regarding Mayur Village in the Malabar District is worth mentioning : "The use of caste titles as surnames by the higher castes served as a verbal identification mark of caste and distinguished them from the lower castes who were not entitled to use surnames. The Brahmins of Madras started the vogue of dropping caste surnames during the anti-Brahmin agitations in that State... But in another respect, there has been considerable standardization in the matter of personal names. All castes in Kerala, the higher more frequently have been replacing Dravidian personal names by Sanskrit names : recently there is a preference for musical names borrowed from Bengal and from films." The decline of traditional economic functions of caste and the rise of modern economic classes are eventful features of change and mobility in caste. A.R. Desai (1959:41:42) thus observes : "The caste system composed of caste groups is a state of increasing decay and undergoing a transformation into modern classes in a confused way and offering stubborn resistance to it, presents the epic spectacle of a social cyclops writhing in violent death agonies."

The family which is the basic and fundamental unit of social structure undergoes, with the passage of time, several changes and modifications. The joint family system which continued to stay for long as the principal feature of the village society is fully disrupted or disintegrated. Its shape and form have immensely diminished and equally its primary functions and obligations have largely changed. It is true that in rural India the joint family still outweighs the elementary or the unitary family, but, for all practical purposes, it is the latter which figures prominently or matters most. There has been a rapid and continuous increase in the number of independent or unitary family, during the last fifteen years. Among the villagers still there prevails a strong attitude towards the elementary type of family and, in that way, the difference on the basis of family types between village and town appears to be redundant.

The family has taken up a new gestalt due to changes in the attitude and aspirations of its members. Extra members of the family who for any reason fail to be accommodated to the agricultural pursuits in the village often find suitable employment outside in town and cities. The break in the economic self-sufficiency of the village promotes a constant exodus of a large number of villagers to these places. A few youngmen, who had their educational training outside the village, particularly prefer to settle over there becauses they don't get such comforts and facilities in the village as are available in towns and cities. Moreover, the solitude of the village combined with stagnation and isolation of social contacts accounts for the growing uneasiness among the youths to settle outside at these places. Migrants are, however, those who are young energetic, though their percentage is still very negligible. The tempo and speed with which the poor and landless labourers move towards the city impinge upon the nature of social dynamics in the village. Migration always brings about disruption in the solidarity of the family bonds and causes a gradual transformation of family relationship from status to contract and from consanguinity to conjugality. Today, the family is stripped off most of its omnibus functions and is transformed into a mere association of the husband, wife and their unmarried children.

The father is no longer an authoritarian figure as the rights and claims of every member are equally honoured and obeyed. If the head of the family is found loosening control or discriminating between the members, his authority is challenged. Misunderstanding with the father or quarrels among brothers and their wives which are the common features of joint living often lead to separation and partition. Defection from traditional norms and values that reinforce family relationship between members of the joint family has largely increased. Moreover, fear of insecurity and dependency has been instrumental in the replacement of the joint family by the unitary one. However, this issue requires further test as the findings of a few sociologists attending the *All-India Conference of Indian Sociologists held last year at Bombay* have not favoured the idea of disintegration in the joint family system in the country.

Practically no significant change is perceptible in the religious and ritualistic behaviour of the villagers. Religion and rituals still exercise powerful influence in shaping the ideology and in guiding the life processes of the people. Except that the ethical side has somewhat changed, its ideological and institutional aspects remain quite intact. The impact of technological and modern materialistic culture has not been so powerful as that of religious culture on the people in this part of the state. The famous *Baidyanath Dham* and *Basukinath Dham*, where large numbers of devotees come from all parts of the country to offer prayers and sacrifices almost every year have been much more influential than the modern scientific, cultural, economic, social, political and the rationalist forces. Religion permeates all activities of the villagers as religious prayers and acts form part of their daily life. The village has seven Sankritan Mandalies in its different Tolas including those of the Harijans. Members of the parties sing devotional songs with harmonium, drum and Kartal at night in the local shrines and thus the whole week is covered by these Mandalies. Notions like Ishwar-Parmeshwar, Swarga-Naraka, Pap-Punya, Dharma-Karma etc. still determine their outlook and shape life destinies. However, the so-called modern and sophisticated youngsters, do not generally conform to these ideals, though the old and the aged still live up to them.

Another significant modern feature which can be taken as a sound basis for an explanation of structural change in the village is expressed in the *economic transformation* of the village. In a wider sense, economic transformations and structural changes are interlinked. The gradual replacement of the old economic system and the institutional machinery by modern and agro-technical or capitalistic institutional channels is a landmark in the annals of economic change in the village. Soon after the advent of national independence, the federal and the State Governments decided to work for the all-round improvement of the peasant communities in India. Plans of Agricultural development became crystallised and machineries to work in rural areas were geared in due course. The role of Community Development project and of Panchayati Raj along with that of voluntary and philanthropic agencies is significant for introducing new changes in the agricultural economy of the villages.

The *Community Development* Block situated at *Amarpur*, which is about six miles away from the village, has undertaken a number of activities with a particular stress on the development of agriculture, animal husbandry, horticulture, health and pisciculture. Frankly admitting the role of C.D. Block complicates the task of proper computation regarding the volume of socio-economic changes, that have taken place independently in the village. However, the present task does not warrant a plea usually taken by social scientists, the complimentary role of the Block has to be taken into consideration while presenting an overall or integrated picture of agricultural and economic changes in the village. A passing reference, without any evaluation, to important development programmes recently introduced by the Block is as under:—

Main Crops :	(1) Paddy, sugercane, wheat, potato and other crops — improved methods of plantation.
	(2) seeds—distribution of improved variety.
	(3) Manure—use of fertilizer, green manures and compost.
	(4) Improved implements—(a) Bihar Junior Plough, (b) Sub Sabash Plough and (c) Japanese weeder.
Plant Protection :	(a) use of hand duster, (b) B.H.C. 5%, (c) D.D.T.O. 25 and (d) hand sprayer
Horticulture :	(a) grafts and gotis for mango, guava, lemon and lichies (b) improved papaya plant.
Pisciculture :	Improved fish-fry
Animal Husbandry :	(a) Haryana bullock, (b) Jamunapari goat (c) veterinary centre (d) innoculation and vaccination against B.Q.R.P.H.S.. (e) fodder development—Napier Juar (f) Castration and (g) artificial insemination.
Poultry :	(a) vaccination against Ranikheta and (b) improved poultry birds—R.I.R. and W.L.H.
Irrigation :	Wells, bundhs, tanks and pumping sets.

Cooperative Societies	:	Multipurpose Cooperative Society, Oil-men's Co-operative Society and Fisher-men's Co-operative Society.

As has already been stated, it is not the concern here to evaluate whether these programmes have been successfully implemented or not. However, it is not denying the fact that the aforesaid activities envisage to bring about radical changes in the agricultural economy of the village.

In the past, the economic structure of the village was based, apart from other things, on the functional interdependence of various castes marked by certain special features like specialised functions, barter system as the convenient and agreeable medium of exchange etc. It is well known that the community's greater confinement to the traditional occupation and sentimental attachment to its settlement near the agricultural land made occupational and physical mobility quite difficult. In fact, some of these traits are still persistent in the village, but as these are unevenly retained among the villagers, it is obvious that these traditional features have today completely disappeared. Artisans and labourers insist on cash payment and mobility is on increase. If a Brahmin takes to an occupation outside the fold of his caste, he is not condemned for such action. The introduction of certain factory-made goods and commodities have mostly weakened certain crafts and industries in the village. The weavers, the carpenters, the smiths, the potters etc. are searching for jobs outside the village.

The most important economic feature of the village in the present time is depicted by what *Sol Tax* calls as penni capitalism in small communities. The village is a small centre of trade and business for the people living in and around it. The farmers often bring their grain and other commodities for sale in the weekly market. The significant point is that the modern economic markets have turned the small and big cultivators into small and big capitalists. Gough (1955 : 43) makes the following observation : "In short, the village is annually participating to an increasing extent in the wider urban economy. This change, everywhere in India, is part of the overall change from a feudal to an expanding capitalist economic system, and is the fundamental prerequisite, in my view, for most other modern changes in the pattern of social relations within the village." However, the emergence of an economic class is still a distant dream to the villagers.

Finally, educational change is a necessary concomitant to the changing ideology and culture of the community. A greater awakening among parents and guardians for the educational and cultural development of their children is there. It is really a pleasant surprise to find quite a large number of children, other than those admitted to the recognized schools, receiving primary education through private tutors at open places in the village. Notwithstanding these efforts for the educational development of the people in the village, a vast number of villagers are still illiterate and ignorant. In the present age, it is needless to emphasize the need and importance of education both for the rural and urban population of the country. The success of democracy depends upon the people who run it, but if the people are mostly illiterate and ignorant, it will not succeed as is the case today. Ramkrishna Mukherjee's suggestion to social scientists is highly remarkable : "Thus the frontiers of the three disciplines do meet in the field of village study", and so scientists duly equipped to cross the no man's land between the disciplines should also be forthcoming. The question, therefore, does not boil down to which discipline should undertake the task or that it can be accomplished only by inter-disciplinary research. Contrariwise, the question throws up the challenge to create interest among those belonging to any one of the disciplines to assume the responsibility and equip themselves accordingly.

ERRATA

Page	*Line*	*Printed*	*Read*
6	16	Maclver	Maciver
8	12	relationship, man	relationship of man
8	29	viilage	village
9	2	certai an	certain
10	17	Sothern	Southern
12	22	K.D. Malviya	H.D. Malviya
16	14	mordern	modern
20	18	Bhorko	Bharko
37	6	in	is
72	2	compartmetalized	compartmentalized
76	2	LAN	LAND
79	12	Frindly	Friendly
82	15	(spares)	(spears)
83	8	grom	*delete*
83	16	the	he
109	1	the	she
114	14	braekup	breakup
122	1	modyfy	modify
139	20	worshipers	worshippers
142	34	belives	believes
145	6	imcluding	including
153	24	writers	writes

INDEX